THE
VISIONARY LEADER

THE
VISIONARY
LEADER

*How Anyone Can Learn
to Lead Better*

✦

JOSEPH M. CHAMPLIN
with CHARLES D. CHAMPLIN

CROSSROAD • NEW YORK

1993
The Crossroad Publishing Company
370 Lexington Avenue, New York, NY 10017

Library of Congress Cataloging-in-Publication Data

Champlin, Joseph M.
   The visionary leader : how anyone can learn to lead better /
Joseph M. Champlin, with Charles D. Champlin.
      p. cm.
   ISBN 0-8245-1235-9 (pbk.)
   1. Christian leadership.   I. Champlin, Charles D.   II. Title.
BV652.1.C48   1993
158'.4—dc20   92-36041
                                                              CIP

Biblical passages are taken from the *New American Bible* Copyright © 1970 by the
confraternity of Christian Doctrine, 3211 Fourth Street, N.E., Washington, D.C. 20017-
1194 and are used with permission. All rights reserved.

Grateful acknowledgment is made to Dominique Lapierre for permission to quote from
his book *The City of Joy* (New York: Warner Books, 1985).

For my stepfather, Charles H. Haynes,
who had an unquenchable thirst
for information about leaders and leadership.

CONTENTS

PREFACE

This book presents three basic points.

1. All of us at some time and in some way influence the thoughts, decisions, or behavior of others. By definition, that makes everyone a leader. Parents immediately come to mind as the foremost examples of this kind of leadership. Yet many people are more likely to think of leaders as the public figures who hold high office or direct large organizations. Thus many readers—for whom this book was written and to whom the concepts in this book most particularly apply—may feel they are not the audience because they hesitate or even refuse to call themselves leaders. But they are.

2. The results of leadership may not show up immediately but only in the future. In their tomorrows, some people will think or act differently because of what a leader said or did today. Teachers are excellent (and admired) examples of people who exert long-term influence. Most of us can easily remember a word, a phrase, a bit of advice, or a gesture of support from a teacher we had years ago—one with whom we may have had absolutely no contact since those elementary or secondary school days. Leaders, and most especially parents and teachers, do touch the future.

3. Certain things—techniques or characteristics—can help anyone become a better and more effective leader, whether it be as a friend or colleague, parent or pastor, corporation CEO or elected official, school administrator or church worker. Philosophers and educators may argue if leaders are born or made and if leadership traits can in fact be actually learned or not. Nevertheless, my deep interest in the subject and considerable experience at several different leadership positions have led me to believe that the dozen qualities discussed in Part II are useful and even critically necessary if one is to lead well. To study, think about, and cultivate those characteristics, and others too, will, I believe, enrich anyone. Those who do so will find they can make better use of qualities that they quite naturally possess in abundance. They may also be able to develop characteristics that they lack, and strengthen those which they have only to a limited degree. I hope that this book will help those who read it to achieve that special kind of personal growth.

ACKNOWLEDGMENTS

I first became seriously interested in the notion of leadership while serving as pastor of Holy Family Church in Fulton, New York, between 1971 and 1979.

The fascination took more concrete form when, in the early 1980s, David Kidd, the principal of the large public high school in Liverpool, New York, invited me to address several dozen high school administrators from the area. I collected some of my ideas into a presentation I called "The Teacher as a Leader." Subsequently I was asked to repeat the talk for various other groups of secular and parochial school leaders. I began to expand my thoughts further in many lectures at gatherings of Roman Catholic clergy and other church personnel around the country. So my first thanks are to David Kidd for setting me on the trail.

At the start of the 1990s, Jim Murphy, the editor of *The Catholic Sun*, the official newspaper of the Syracuse diocese, asked me to write a weekly column. I called the column "Touching the Future" and started to put some of my ideas about leadership into print.

The idea of interviewing specific leaders and using their stories to illustrate various aspects of leadership occurred to me as I was doing the columns for the *Sun*. During the summer and fall of 1991, with tape recorder in hand, I visited each of the twelve leaders I've written about in Part II of this book.

The year-long writing of "Touching the Future" became the

groundwork for *The Visionary Leader*, and portions of the columns, as well as the interviews, have found their way into the book. So my second note of thanks is to Jim Murphy and his associate Jeff Charbonneau for their encouragement.

I was excited by the interviews and even more by the willingness of busy people such as Henry Mancini not only to grant me the interview but later to read and comment on the written versions (Mr. Mancini changed one word). I was less happy with the interviews as written: I'd had neither the training nor the experience in what was essentially a form of journalism.

That's when my brother Charles entered the picture. After graduating from Harvard he spent seventeen years as a reporter and writer with *Time* and *Life* magazines and more than twenty-six years as arts editor and columnist with the *Los Angeles Times*. Now retired from the newspaper, my brother is still a working journalist in both print and television. I asked if he would edit this book. He quickly consented, but with the proviso that his suggestions would only be that, and final decisions were mine. I agreed.

The collaboration has been a wonderful experience for me, and I think for both of us: two brothers now in their sixties working together for the first time on a project that occasionally touches their personal roots. I am terribly grateful for his help, and for this special bonding in our lives. Perhaps surprisingly (or perhaps not) we had no squabbles, although there were some heavy discussions about Chapters 9 and 10. The result was a major rewriting of both sections with—in our opinions—significant improvements in both.

We have brought different experiences to the book, he as an editor, I as a priest. He is married and the father of six children; I am an uncle ten times and, at this moment, great-uncle nine times. Although Charles lives in Los Angeles, and I live in upstate New York, we are always in close contact. Our last serious argument was whether to see Harry James (his choice) or visit a model train exhibit (my choice) at the 1939 World's Fair in New York, when he was thirteen and I was nine. (My memory is that our wise single-parent mother somehow scheduled it so we did both.) Since then I recall no major battles between us, and this collaboration has been singularly enthusiastic and peaceful.

The revising of works of fiction customarily involves only the writer, possibly his or her agent, and certainly the editor. But I have found that works of nonfiction are often much improved and enriched by a wider consultation. The process presumes the writer's openness to criticism and her or his willingness to change. The writer risks the sting of hard criticism or the danger of superficial and deceiving praise. But always in my experience the crucible of criticism makes for a better book in the end. As pages like this always say, the book remains the author's responsibility and its shortcomings, too, are hers or his. But for all those named here who have read and commented on the manuscript, I am most genuinely grateful.

These include a half-dozen readers who gave me useful direction as I began and valuable specific comments when I finished. I thank Brad Broadwell, Ann Ferro, Father Phil Murnion, Sharon O'Connell, Dr. Rudy Rubeis, and Margaret O'Brien Steinfels.

Many friends and colleagues have offered helpful suggestions here and there. Thus my thanks are due as well to Donald Brophy; Lawrence Bordt, C.S.P.; my sister-in-law Peggy Champlin, Chuck's wife of more than forty years; Michael Donovan; James Hayes; Jeffrey Keefe; John and Carol Lawyer; Michael Meagher; Bishop James Malone; Chris Phillips; Neal Quartier; William Regan; John Roark; Stephen Rossetti; Sister Mary Xavier McKenna, D.C.; the staff at St. Joseph's parish in Camillus, including my partner Father John Broderick; and Tom Zedar. My thanks to all of them—and to anyone I have inadvertently overlooked.

I am very grateful to Michael Leach, the publisher of Crossroad books, whose constructive and enthusiastic encouragement meant much to me during the low moments that befall the writer of any book. And to Ellen Gordon for her careful copy editing.

As she has for a dozen years, Patricia Gale has deciphered my difficult handscript (I am a too rapidly writing southpaw) and put it into the word processor with a wonderful blend of patience and ingenuity. I give her my heartfelt thanks. Lastly, I give my thanks to Maureen Suatoni, who with fine efficiency put the final draft of the book into the hands of my several commentators and of the interviewees themselves.

The bottom line, as they say in my brother's sphere of coverage, is my prayerful hope that these pages will help those who read them become ever more effective leaders.

JOSEPH M. CHAMPLIN
Camillus, New York

PART I

◆

EVERYONE
IS A LEADER

1

PARENTS ESPECIALLY

Millions hear and like the music of Henry Mancini.

His talents and efforts have given pleasure to countless listeners, provided employment for many musicians, and inspired numerous artists. In addition, the scholarships Mancini has established at several universities and music schools across the United States have opened the way for talented young people to develop their own gifts and become tomorrow's composers, arrangers, and conductors.

But Henry Mancini, the private man, has also been married for nearly forty-five years. He and his wife Ginny have worked hard to be successful at bringing up their son and twin daughters.

Who has exerted the greater impact upon others—Henry Mancini the musician, or Henry Mancini the father? Who has touched others more deeply, the composer and conductor, or the spouse and parent?

This is an interesting and perhaps thought provoking, but clearly unanswerable question.

The executive vice president of an eastern seaboard pharmaceutical company would not hazard a response to that inquiry. However, as the father of a half-dozen children, he didn't hesitate to comment: "I have been in the corporate world all my life and held many top, tough positions. But every one of those jobs was a piece of cake compared to raising six children."

The national sales manager for a Florida-based international plastics manufacturing firm goes a step further. "Hey, these jobs are a piece of cake compared to raising *three* children."

Moreover, he credits his wife for any success they have enjoyed in their parenting roles, and he labels her a leader. "She is the real leader in the family. She keeps us working together, staying focused and moving ahead."

He calls his wife a leader. Most would say the same of Henry Mancini. But who is a leader? What does it mean to lead?

Defining Terms

One dictionary uses a full page of text for defining *to lead* and *leader*. The following definitions serve our purpose well and set the tone of this book.

"*Lead*: to guide on a way; show the way to a place, especially by going with or in advance . . . To guide by indicating the way; mark out or show the way."

"*Leader*: a person who by force of example, talents or qualities of leadership plays a deciding role, wields commanding influence or has a following in any sphere of activity or thought."[1]

This dictionary cites more than a dozen examples of leaders: A conductor or leading performer of a musical ensemble, the first or foremost person in a file or advising body, a person who directs a class, an adult responsible for guidance of a scout troop, a skilled employee who supervises one or more groups of workers.

Curiously, this dictionary omits mentioning parents as prime illustrations of leaders or leadership or leading.

A Curious Phenomenon

Perhaps it is not so curious that a dictionary omits parents as prime illustrations of persons who lead. I have found that most people do not see themselves as leaders. Most have an extremely restricted vision of what leadership means; most see the label "leader" as applying only to very public persons such as the pope or the president, a commanding general of the armed forces, or a corporation's chief executive officer.

Even teachers, as we see in the next chapter, may hesitate to be called leaders, and some have been wary of workshops entitled "The Teacher as Leader."

But if we accept the dictionary definition of leader, is not every person, at some moments and with some people, a leader? If we embrace the concept that a leader "by example, talents or qualities plays a deciding role, wields commanding influence or has a following in any sphere of activity or thought," doesn't this mean that every human being, at least occasionally, exerts a leadership role, whether in the lives of one other person or several?

A friend influences a friend. A police officer plays a deciding role in the direction drivers take. A receptionist creates a relaxed and cordial or a tense and hostile atmosphere for those in the waiting room. A nurse aids all those on a floor of the hospital— physically and, even more, emotionally. A doctor has hundreds who follow her or his minute medical directions. An office manager, construction superintendent, factory supervisor, or store owner daily directs the lives of a few or many people. If we agree with our dictionary definition, this list of examples clearly is endless.

It is true that few of these leaders make the cover of *Time* or *Newsweek*. It is likewise true that when we use the word *leader* in ordinary conversation, we are usually referring to highly visible people in positions of power and responsibility, whose decisions affect a large number of others. Nevertheless, is it not true that everyone, even if on a lesser level and involving fewer persons, is a leader?

And if this is true, then aren't parents the largest leadership group of all? Are not parents surely the first leaders in all of our lives? Indeed, are not parents likely to have not only the earliest but also the most lasting influences on our lives? Is it not true, now as ever, that a child's thinking and behavior are shaped most decisively by the examples the parents set?

Parenting and Parents

This book is not directly about parenting, but one way or another parents loom large in it. Each one of the leaders discussed in Part II bears the influence of her or his parents. The vignettes of the leaders' lives often reveal specific ways in which their dads and moms affected their lives.

The mother of former CBS head Tom Wyman helped him sift out the relative value of athletics and academics, and encouraged him to excel in his collegiate studies. The director of Catholic Charities, Sister Charla Commins, learned invaluable lessons about helping others—from parents who were constantly sharing the limited resources they had with others in need.

Lecturer and educator Patricia Livingston absorbed the value of listening from a mother who was skilled in the art of listening. From her lawyer father who served as judge advocate general of the army, she acquired an eagerness for every facet of life. Chief County Executive Officer Jack Plumley repeatedly heard during his earliest days his parents' comments that if he did the best he could, he was as good as anyone else, even if he did not have as much or had not achieved as well as others. Without even knowing the phrase, his parents were instilling within their son the basis for a healthy self-esteem that would positively impact on his later political life.

Most of these leaders are also parents. Like Mancini, they have sought to raise their children well. Like all fathers and mothers they have struggled in the process, wondering what to say or do and how to say or do it. AMTRAK Executive Vice President William Norman is anxious about his young daughter at college or his son in a Catholic high school. My niece Susan tries to balance a career writing for *Modern Maturity* and mothering her tiny firstborn infant. Housewife, spouse, and mother Kathy Bernardi seeks the wisdom of understanding when to correct and when to praise her young daughter and son. Philadelphia Phillies General Manager Lee Thomas is on his second go-round of child rearing and can draw on some previous experience with his two young sons.

Most of us like stories or examples. We also can learn much from lived experiences, our own and those of others. Although this book was not conceived or completed as a treatise on parenting, many lessons about parenting are nevertheless woven into the vignettes of the thirteen leaders whose lives are sketched at the beginning of each chapter. The accounts of how their parents influenced them and how they now influence their own children are teaching tools in themselves.

If we agree that everyone is a leader—particularly parents— then the characteristics of effective leaders discussed in Part II apply to fathers and mothers as well. The examination of those dozen qualities should help them because what makes better leaders necessarily makes better parents.

Questions for Reflection:

1. Can you identify some specific ways in which your parents have influenced your attitudes, thoughts, and behavior?
2. If you are a parent, can you recognize some specific ways in which you have influenced your child or children?

2

TEACHERS, TOO, TOUCH THE FUTURE

When Christa McAuliffe took off in the doomed Challenger capsule, she carried with her a T-shirt presented to her by her students at Concord High School in New Hampshire. McAuliffe was to be the "first teacher in space," and her pupils had decorated the hallways of that New England building with many banners, one of which read: "Go, Christa. Reach for the Stars."

The gift T-shirt carried this simple message: "I touch the future. I teach."

Teachers Touch the Future

Teachers do touch the future. They prepare pupils for tomorrow, influence their way of thinking, help students make choices that will chart their years ahead, and leave them with lessons which last a lifetime.

I know that from my own experiences.

• One day during French class when I was a student at Camden (New York) Central School, an attractive female classmate seated at the adjoining desk began to flirt with me while the instructor was writing on the blackboard with her back to us. I rather enjoyed my classmate's overtures and I flirted right back.

Then I caught sight of Mrs. Poole, my math teacher, out in

the hall peering through the room's door windows and clearly disapproving our adolescent goings-on.

When the bell rang and class ended, this redheaded wife of a naval officer on duty in the Pacific (these were World War II days) confronted me in the corridor. I shifted uneasily and made some silly explanations about my behavior. Without a moment's pause she bore right in and said quite sharply, "Joe, anyone can make excuses."

That was over forty years ago. I haven't seen Mrs. Poole nor heard from or about her since I left high school. But that moment and her words—all too true—are etched forever in my memory.

• I completed my last year of secondary school at Phillips Academy in Andover, Massachusetts. Emory Basford, an English teacher there and our dormitory "housemaster," regularly hosted a required Sunday afternoon tea session for his young residents. I can remember almost nothing else about those gatherings, yet one thing Mr. Basford said has had a tremendous impact on my life.

"Gentlemen," he once said, "Don't waste your precious morning hours on light reading like newspapers and magazines. Use that time for serious study and work. Leave the lighter material for later periods when you have less energy."

I had no contact with Mr. Basford after I graduated from Andover in 1947. He died only recently in his ninety-first year, having taught at Andover from 1929 until 1964. But the warning advice he gave us nearly five decades ago is still an operative principle for me. Since then I have written thirty-five books, composed some one thousand columns, and prepared countless homilies or talks. I did all this writing during my "precious" fresh moments, always between 8:00–10:00 in the morning and never late at night.

Both Mrs. Poole and Mr. Basford touched my future with those sharp precepts. As teachers, they were, in fact, leaders.

Reluctant Leaders

What is almost certainly true is that only parents are more influential than teachers in shaping our society. Educators surely fulfill the definitions of leaders and leadership noted in the last chapter. They guide, mark out, or show the way. They play a deciding role, wield commanding influence, and they have a following. Yet I have discovered that teachers often squirm when someone calls them leaders. If they accept the label, they accept it reluctantly.

In preparing an all-morning workshop on leadership for over 300 teachers of the West Genesee Public School District in Camillus, New York, I sat down a month in advance with six faculty members to plan the session. The committee had already sent up trial balloons announcing the topic and soliciting impressions or suggestions from the teachers. To my surprise, there were several negative reactions to a workshop entitled "The Teacher as Leader."

Why was there such hostility or at least hesitation to this linking of teacher and leader? Apparently the teachers, already feeling heavily burdened (and not without reason), worried that leadership would entail additional responsibilities for them.

They asked: Does this mean we should be explaining *Robert's Rules of Order*? Are we supposed to be training students in parliamentary procedure? Is our goal to graduate only future elected officials or governmental employees? Are we expected to be social activists or run for a political post?

They seemed to fail initially to recognize or to accept the truth that as teachers they were already leaders by the nature of their profession. They do indeed touch the future by leading their students toward tomorrow.

Another Definition of Leadership

A less formal and more poetic definition of a leader then could be: A leader is someone who touches another's future.

Leaders affect the direction a person or a group will take. They influence the shape, the thrust, the future of an individual or a community, a family or a school, a church or a nation. They guide us into the world ahead.

In a true sense, everyone is a leader sometime—in some way

affecting the life of someone else, perhaps of several someones. Each of us touches the future of others.

I have found during a dozen workshops that once this notion of leadership was spelled out, the reluctance of teachers to acknowledge their roles as leaders vanished. The teachers also became keenly interested in the characteristics of a good leader—the topic I treat in Part II.

Questions for Reflection
1. Are you able to recall individual teachers who influenced you or touched your future?
2. In what particular manner did they do so?

3

CLERGY AND OTHER CHURCH PERSONNEL

My fascination with the topic of leadership actually began during the 1960s and has continued ever since. This on-going interest continually brings me to the same questions. Who are contemporary leaders in the world today? How did they achieve that status? Can we identify certain common characteristics of good, effective leadership?

Five facets of my own life have fueled this fascination.

1. *Pastoring a parish.* I have spent roughly half of these last three decades as the pastor of Roman Catholic churches in up-state New York. One was a moderate-size parish, 750 families, in the small city of Fulton, and the other, a relatively large parish, 1500 families, in the suburban Syracuse community of Camillus. Those experiences gave me repeated lessons in guiding a group of people with very diverse backgrounds, attitudes, and needs. They also taught me the importance of tapping into the talents of the church's members, of developing motivational approaches and practical techniques to foster volunteerism among parishioners.

2. *Serving in church administration.* I spent the other half of those decades working in Catholic Church administration. From 1968 to 1971 I served on the national level as associate director of the Liturgy Office for the National Conference of Catholic Bishops in Washington. During most of the 1980s I held the position of vicar for Parish Life and Worship in my own diocese

of Syracuse. These two administrative posts made me more directly aware of what makes large organizations function effectively and why good communication skills are critically important for any type of leader.

3. *Lecturing here and abroad.* At that time, thirty years ago, when the issue of leadership first began to fascinate me, I also began an unexpected and unplanned secondary career as a lecturer. Those speaking engagements took me on more than a million miles of travel at home and abroad. I visited every area of the United States, with trips as well to Canada, Panama, Europe, and South Africa. This was a period of enormous upheaval in the Catholic Church and my presentations usually centered around some aspect of those changes.

The audiences were generally clergy and other interested or involved Catholics. Invitations to lecture came unsolicited, and I accepted them as long as they did not interfere with my primary responsibilities as parish pastor or church administrator.

These journeys brought me to many special locations, enabled me to interact with over 30,000 priests or deacons, and put me in contact with great numbers of laypersons. For example, I am presently writing these words in spectacularly beautiful Banff, Alberta, during the afternoon break of a four-day seminar with seventy-five priests and their bishop from Calgary, Canada. We are exploring some of the weighty challenges facing the North American Catholic Church as it prepares to enter the next millennium.

Those travel/lecture experiences have combined to create a rich reservoir of inspiration, ideas, and information for me. Several specific concepts and practical illustrations from that treasury appear in the pages that follow. However, the dominant notions that I have absorbed from these encounters are the complexities connected with any attempts to modify human behavior, and the courage required to lead people from where they are to where they are not.

4. *Reading around the topic.* I have read over a dozen books about leaders and leadership. Some have treated the subject theoretically, such as the well-known *Megatrends, One Minute Manager,* and *In Search of Excellence.* These texts concentrated on

providing general principles, even though they cited concrete examples in support of their recommendations.

Other books examined the lives of individuals who exercise leadership roles in the world today. They included persons in both the religious and secular fields, as widely varied as Lee Iacocca and Mother Teresa, Pope John XXIII and Donald Trump.

I came to recognize from my readings just how essential it is for any leader to have a vision. I also found some pragmatic suggestions for promoting harmonious relationships among those with whom you are working.

5. *Speaking about leadership.* During the 1980s I pulled together into lecture form some of the notions I had accumulated over these years through reading and reflecting on leaders and leadership. The combined ideas were first presented as an after-dinner talk during a monthly meeting of local public school administrators. They seemed to react quite positively to the concepts and the approach. At least their subsequent recommendations led to a dozen workshops or keynote addresses on the subject for area educators such as teachers and middle managers in a variety of secular school systems. Later I made similar presentations to Catholic clergy, pastoral ministers, teachers, and religious educators in different parts of this country and Canada. The positive response to these lectures encouraged me to think about a book on leadership.

I have written these words from my perspective and experience as a Roman Catholic priest, one who has held both pastoral and administrative positions in the church. The concepts in this book have been helpful to me and seemed to have been useful for the staff members of those parishes and offices in which I have worked. I trust that they may prove equally valuable for the clergy and church personnel in Catholic parishes, agencies, and offices. It is my hope that leaders in other religious traditions will likewise find merit in these ideas.

Questions for Reflection

1. Have you been inspired by recognized leaders in the church, clergy, or otherwise?
2. How did they impact you?

4

WORKERS IN
THE MARKETPLACE

Not all teachers labor full time and in formal classroom settings. Some are part-time employees; some are volunteers. Some, moreover, instruct in the religious education field. For them the teaching goal is twofold: to prepare students for better lives in the years ahead on this earth and also to prepare them for a life still to come in the next world.

Every one of these teachers can be considered a leader who touches the future of others. There is, of course, a unique dimension to the leadership given by teachers of religion. Some of these part-time educators have double roles as leaders—both in their teaching and in their jobs.

Walter Gilroy was one of those individuals, a full-time worker and a part-time church leader. Short and thin, reserved and soft-spoken, Walter never gained acclaim as a charismatic, forceful, and renowned leader either in church or at work. But after his sudden death, the evidence of the impact Walter had had in life surfaced in remarkable ways.

Walter was married and was the father of several children. He held a middle-management position at the Sylvania GTE plant near our parish buildings. He and I jogged together now and again. He gave me some useful criticisms about a manuscript on prayer that I was writing. In appreciation I gave him a copy of *Christian Prayer*, an official Roman Catholic book of formal prayers. From that abbreviated version of the full *Liturgy of the Hours*, Walter began to recite Morning and Evening Prayer faithfully each day. He regularly participated at a weekday morning Mass, taught religion classes for teenagers, and eventually became an active member of the Rite for Christian Initiation team who worked with adults seeking to enter the Catholic Church.

Then, during a vacation in his native New England, Walter collapsed one day while he was running along the Atlantic beach. Unfortunately, serious brain damage occurred before he could be revived. The family clan kept prayerful vigil at the hospital bedside of their silent spouse and father for the four days before he died.

Aware of his custom of morning and evening prayer, they recited together the words in Walter's stead. One daughter remembered the rosary from her religious education classes of long ago. She taught the others, and led them all in praying the beads. Everyone at some point held Walter's hand and caressed his forehead, while speaking words of faith and love into his ears.

On the night before his burial from a Rhode Island church, Walter's fellow employees at the Camillus GTE plant made a twelve-hour round-trip by chartered bus to the funeral home. They made that long journey just to be able to spend a few moments offering their condolences to the family and their respects to a colleague whom they loved and admired.

A week later at St. Joseph's Church I celebrated a memorial Mass for this quiet man whose profound influence was truly amazing. More than 200 employees walked up the hill from GTE to our church for the liturgy.

It was relatively easy to gather material for the homily, but quite difficult to deliver it. I had, of course, my own memories of him, but I picked up additional information about Walter from his neighbors and his colleagues at work. The night before I sat for an hour at his house with his wife and children listening to their own recollections.

The homily simply brought out some of Walter Gilroy's positive characteristics—his prayerfulness, his dedicated efforts as a parish religion instructor, and his obvious impact upon the workers at GTE. I also related some family incidents, including a few humorous ones. I cited the remarkable chartered bus venture—such an expenditure of money, time, and energy for just those few moments at a funeral home—and described his days at the hospital surrounded by people who loved him in a special way.

The homily then linked the admirable life of this man to the church's faith and biblical hope in personal resurrection and ultimate reunion. "At a Catholic Christian funeral we don't say 'good-bye, Walter,' but instead, 'until we meet again.'"

Afterward, a participant and coworker wrote me a letter including these comments:

> I attended the Memorial Mass today for Walter Gilroy. You may remember that we spoke briefly after the service, but I just have to take a few minutes to further express my thoughts and to tell you how much your message meant not only to me but many of my friends that work here at GTE. Some of us worked with Walt and many others of us were touched by him and his giving graceful self.
>
> All things you said are so true of him. But your service and sermon went beyond an excellent eulogy and beautiful music. You strengthened my—our faith in the Lord and my spirit was renewed, and I found myself responding to the Lord through your message. I wish to say thank you for making Jesus real to us even as you spoke of our dear friend and brother in Christ, Walter Gilroy.
>
> I may not be a Catholic, but as a fellow believer, I hold in esteem and sacred the expressions we all make toward a closer walk with Jesus.
>
> When we came back to the office, many of us gathered in small groups. You could tell we had experienced being in God's presence during Mass.
>
> I know we all were strengthened today in our faith.

Walter Gilroy was clearly a leader. He deeply touched the future of many, not only as a spouse and parent but also as a caring worker in the business world and as an active member of his parish church.

Some Other Leaders

Every chapter in Part II of this book begins with the story of a person who, like Walter Gilroy, has touched the future of others. Those quite diverse leaders include:

Six men, five women, one couple;

Eight who are Catholic and five who are not;

Some who are in full-time religion work, some part-time church volunteers and some perhaps not affiliated with any religious body;

Two from Florida, three from the East Coast, four from central New York, one from the Midwest, and three from the West Coast;

Some who are well known publicly (e.g., Mancini and Mahony), others who are known mostly in their one area of expertise (e.g., Thomas and Livingston), still others who are known only in a smaller circle of relatives, friends, and colleagues (e.g., Bernardi and Panebianco).

Leadership Qualities

Each one of these persons possesses a number of notable and admirable leadership qualities. However, during my interviews I concentrated only upon a single characteristic of the individual that seemed to emerge in a strong way during our dialogue. For example, Francis and Barbara Scholtz from Jacksonville, Florida, find quiet time each morning for biblical reading and prayerful reflection; Pam Panebianco has displayed great determination and trust in following and communicating to others a challenging method of responsible parenthood.

The personal interviews were exciting for me; I hope the written account proves interesting for readers. They are intended only to set a tone and offer a living example of the specific characteristic under consideration.

The balance of each chapter provides general principles, useful suggestions, and practical illustrations of the quality being examined.

This book emerges from my perspective and experience as a

Roman Catholic priest. However, during those presentations on leadership to audiences of mixed religious and nonreligious backgrounds, the concepts and stories appeared sufficiently universal in scope to be both understandable, engaging, and helpful for them. My hope is, and efforts have been, to make these written words prove equally so.

Questions for Reflection
1. Who are some leaders you admire today?
2. What leadership characteristics do they seem to possess?

PART II

♦

HOW ANYONE
CAN LEARN
TO LEAD BETTER

ROLE MODELS, GENERAL PRINCIPLES, USEFUL SUGGESTIONS, AND PRACTICAL ILLUSTRATIONS

"Leaders are not born, nor are they made—they are self-made.

"There are simply no such things as 'leadership traits' or 'leadership characteristics.' Of course, some people are better leaders than others. By and large, though, we are talking about skills that perhaps cannot be taught but they can be learned by most of us. True, some people genuinely cannot learn the skills. They may not be important to them; or they'd rather be followers. But most of us can learn them."

—Peter F. Drucker, *Managing the Non-Profit Organization*[1]

1

Vision

Above all else, good leaders are visionaries. They see beyond what is to what might be, could be, ought to be. They imagine the possibilities, recognize the potential. But, more than that, they inspire others to dream along with them. Together, the leaders and their colleagues shape their individual hopes and aspirations into a single vision for tomorrow. Then, with the dream defined, the leader reinforces it again and again, urging and stimulating everyone to sustain the effort until the dream becomes a reality.

William S. Norman
Executive Vice President of AMTRAK

Some of the leaders in this book had a clear vision from their earliest years of what they wished to be and do when they grew up. For example, Lee Thomas was constantly carrying around his bat and glove when he was still in first grade and Henry Mancini began playing the flute when he was only eight. Both were already dreaming of lifelong careers in baseball and music. Throughout their childhood days and beyond, each of them spent all the time they could pursuing goals they saw in their mind's eye. They knew where they wanted to go.

That wasn't the way it was for William Norman. Norman, the son of a Norfolk, Virginia, carpenter, spent his childhood years in the black section of that southern city.

"We were poor, but didn't know it, since everyone in the neighborhood shared the same situation," Norman says. "My parents never attended college, but they were affectionate, caring and they urged us to be the best we were capable of being."

"I loved to read," Norman remembers, "even though I was not a bookworm. I enjoyed the Bible, especially the Psalms, not so much for the religious aspect but because of their literary beauty. I went to summer Bible school voluntarily for nine years in a row, but more for the socialization."

"During those days, my ideas or dreams about the future were not very clear. I was a good student, but the only role model was one member of our community who came back to us as a lawyer. So I thought of being a lawyer."

When it came time for college, however, Norman understood that with an older sister already at a university, he could not expect any financial help from his parents. Consequently, he selected a school, not because he could take a prelaw major, but because the school offered scholarship help. He chose the college, West Virginia Wesleyan, which provided him the greatest "delta," as he calls it—an institution where the gap between the total cost and the scholarship was the smallest.

Actually, Norman did not study law there. "Those were the mid-50s when, because of concern about space exploration, sciences were the 'in' subject," he says. "I majored instead in chemistry and mathematics with a minor in physics and German. After graduation, I taught for a few months in the Norfolk public school system before resigning to accept a U.S. Navy Commission."

His naval career (1961–73) was diverse and distinguished: flight officer, Pentagon Air Weapons Systems analyst, instructor at the Naval Academy, graduate student, combat duty in Southeast Asia, special assistant to the chief of Naval Operations.

"The navy was good to me," Norman acknowledges, "but after about seven years I decided to reenter the civilian field and I submitted a letter of resignation. However, in this letter I pointed out that the navy needed to do a better job at integrating minorities and women into its operation, not out of any altruistic motives, but simply because it was wasting an enormous amount of talent and energy through its exclusionary practices. My resignation letter and attachment detailing all this and more became almost a book and ran on for twenty-four pages."

To his surprise, the newly appointed chief of Naval Operations, Admiral E. R. Zumwalt, Jr., quickly responded and offered him a challenge to do something about it.

"As you can probably surmise already," Norman said to me, "I am intrigued by a challenge. I accepted the invitation. For the next three years we were able to achieve some good things in this area." One especially satisfying project also led to a position he was soon to assume in the civilian sector.

"We were engaged in a tripartite enterprise. A black community on the West Coast had a polluted water supply system. We were able to combine efforts by the Navy Seabees, the local community, and an enlightened corporation—the Cummins Engine Company of Columbus, Indiana—to remedy that situation. I was so impressed by the leadership at Cummins that I later joined them, eventually becoming vice president of the Eastern Division, with offices at Westport, Connecticut."

His successful six-year stint at Cummins attracted the notice of executive "headhunters." The president of AMTRAK, who was looking for a topflight marketing leader, learned about Norman through a headhunter and prevailed upon him to join the National Railroad Passenger Corporation in its Washington headquarters.

Why, in 1979, would this remarkably articulate man take a cut in pay to join an organization with a rather dismal past and a dim future?

"I was fascinated by this challenge," Norman responded. "There were any number of reasons not to take this job. Here was an organization that was sort of stumbling along. It was having unbelievable problems marketing its products. It wasn't receiving the customer reception it should have had. It was not generating a profit. It had dilapidated equipment and wasn't able to give the kind of customer service it wanted to give. And here was an organization that basically had been set up to fail.

"They said to me, 'We are in need of a turnaround and feel that you are the person to do it. Are you interested in coming with us?'

"I said to Alan Boyd, the president of AMTRAK at the time, 'I can't think of one good reason for coming. There is a smaller compensation package; there is an almost impossible business situation here; and there is insufficient support except for a belief that AMTRAK like others is the little engine that can.'"

But Boyd had a vision that stirred William Norman. The corporation's president was convinced of the importance of AMTRAK for the national railroad system in the United States. He also believed strongly that, despite the great difficulties under which AMTRAK began and under which it was operating, it would succeed.

"Here was an opportunity of immense proportions," Norman says, "but Alan Boyd did not believe it could be achieved without a change in the direction that we were moving. And that redirection would require not just a series of incidental steps, but some quantum leaps. He was convinced it could happen if he could get the kind of team around him to help bring this vision to reality.

"It was, quite frankly," Norman admits, "the sincerity of Alan Boyd, a wonderful human being, and the pride, the belief that this could be done, that here was a challenge and an opportunity crying out to be achieved, which attracted me."

It was not an easy decision. The question of money, his family obligations, and the trauma of a move weighed on Norman's mind. "But I rationalized, arguing to myself that I should do this out of a sense of service to the country and agreed to stay only eighteen months to try to achieve the turnaround."

Once he was settled in, Norman summoned staff and line personnel and launched his "Sixty-Day Project," a brainstorming effort to gather every conceivable marketing idea for AMTRAK's future. These were weeks of dreaming.

Norman urged employees to submit any concept, however seemingly wild or impractical. Toward the end of this visionary process, they sifted through the suggestions and compiled a massive 100-point plan, "Marketing in the 80s."

Norman presented the comprehensive document to Alan Boyd on New Year's Eve. He asked for the AMTRAK president's approval of the concept and for the authority (and that meant both money and personnel) to carry it through. Boyd gave him both.

One of the visionary marketing steps was to invest $54 million for a computer reservation and information system that was compatible with the ones used by travel agents. Another major move was to gain membership in the Airline Reporting Corporation. Today AMTRAK has 40,000 approved travel agents as opposed to 4,000 in 1979, and they account for 40 percent of sales—proving the soundness of those two suggestions alone.

Norman attributes the success of that plan—all 100 items were at least underway by 1982—to its ownership by AMTRAK employees. He judged that the vision or dream had actually been lying dormant in the minds of most who worked at the office. His Sixty Day Project and the resulting document simply brought those ideas to the forefront and gained instantaneous acceptance by all involved.

Where is William Norman now? He is still at AMTRAK, but is now executive vice president. New challenges continue to intrigue him and the eighteen-month agreement keeps on being renewed. In the meantime, Norman goes on dreaming impossible dreams and stimulating those around him to have their own dreams of the AMTRAK future. They are already sketching a vision for AMTRAK in the next century.

A picture of his two teenage children hangs on the wall of Norman's office in the handsomely renovated Washington Union Station. His daughter is wearing her cheerleader's outfit and his son is wearing a football uniform. Living in a comfortable McLean, Virginia, home, his children certainly do not know the poverty their father experienced in his childhood years and they probably have not known the same degree of prejudice he suffered. But they do know what it is to have affectionate, caring parents who are urging them to become all they are capable of.

"My father died recently," Norman said, "and during these last days with him I understood very clearly that he always cared deeply for us and tried to be the best parent he could. I am trying to do the same.

"My daughter is sixteen, has good grades, is very popular, into all kinds of activities, but soon will be off to college and I worry about how she is going to do there at her young age. My fifteen-year-old son—well, he is a fine young man interested in everything except academics. So we have decided after careful reflection and advice to transfer him to a parochial school. This worries us, too. We are Episcopalians, but hope that the stricter discipline and regimen in a Catholic high school will help him develop in a more balanced way and that this is the best thing for him.

"We want our children to know they have our support," Norman explains, "that we have high expectations for them and urge them to be better. Quite candidly, this is not leadership; this is just trying to care about our children, trying to instill the best values we can, trying to show them good example and then to hope for the best."

William Norman did not have a clear vision of his own future, but he responded to and has made the most of all his opportunities and challenges. And his two children, including the son now probably more interested in the Washington Redskins than in English literature, will be better prepared for the future, thanks to the role models their father and grandfather have been for them.[1]

For all his brilliance, William Norman has missed a major point. He and his wife have been constantly urging their two adolescent children to become all they are capable of being. They have been holding out high expectations for them and encouraging their daughter and son to be better. Yet Norman apologizes, as it were, and claims that this is not leadership, but only parents doing the best that they can.

The fact is, however, that a major, an essential, perhaps even the most important task of any leader is to be a person with vision. Mr. and Mrs. Norman have offered, repeatedly and with love, just that to their children—a vision of their tomorrows, a portrait of what they can become, a sketch of future possibilities for them. Contrary to Norman's disclaimer, they both have been real leaders in their parenting roles.

Visionary Leaders

In the fall of 1987, Americans were dazed by seizures and collapses on stock markets around the world. As *Time* magazine phrased it, a door to the future had been blown open and what the world saw seemed frightening.

People looked to the White House for both "substance and symbol to announce that the most powerful office in the world was alive to the danger." The country urgently needed focus, intelligence, communication, and an adult voice who would offer a hopeful vision of tomorrow.

Spokespersons across the nation in both the media and the government unanimously cried out for the moment's most pressing commodity: "Leadership! Leadership!"[2]

The leaders called for would first and foremost need to be individuals with a vision of the future. But that kind of vision as mentioned previously, is a requisite for every leader. Parents and pastors, bishops and bureaucrats—all must have it.

Parents, as the Normans have done, must cling to and hold up for children a vision of what their potential really is and who they can truly become.

This task is surely difficult for parents when confused and rebellious adolescents seem destined for disaster instead of bound for glory. As one very successful late bloomer told me recently, "I was a terrible teenager, an incredible burden to my folks. I fell in with a bad crowd and paid the price. My parents suffered greatly through those years."

Pastors must present over and over again a vision of what under God's grace the parish can be. That pictured future often will move the flock into unfamiliar and uncomfortable territory.

For example, two close clerical colleagues directed the renovation of their churches during the past few years. This was a most challenging task, one requiring wisdom, patience, courage, and, above all, a clear vision of what tomorrow's building would look like.

Bishops must facilitate the development of a vision for their dioceses and then convey that to the thousands of Catholics for whom they are responsible.

Sister Sharon Euart, RSM, works in Washington, D.C., for the American bishops as the associate general secretary of United States Catholic Conference. She notes that after Vatican II the church experienced a new vision and a renewed sense of purpose. However, carrying out that vision and projecting that sense of purpose have been slow, tedious, and not always successful enterprises.

She presently helps guide the U.S. Catholic bishops' planning efforts. These processes are intended to develop a mission statement, major goals, and specific objectives for a three-year period. That means both creating a view of the future and establishing practical ways of transforming this dream into a reality.

Bureaucrats—or, more precisely, people in governmental or institutional positions—must likewise possess and project a vision of greatness for their municipality, state, country, company, corporation, and even the world.

Mikhail Gorbachev made *perestroika* (restructuring) and *glasnost* (openness) words that most non-Russian-speaking people now understand. President F. W. de Klerk opened a prison door and gave all South Africans hope for peace with justice in their troubled land. George Bush spoke of the thousand points of light initiative and stimulated a further development of volunteerism in the United States.

By its nature, vision is futuristic. In contrast, most people probably prefer the here and now or the way it always has been. Leaders thus must either capitulate to their constituents' complacency or win them over to their own dream of a better tomorrow. Henry Kissinger summarizes those challenges of being a visionary in these words: "The task of the leader is to get his people from where they are to where they have not been. The public does not fully understand the world into which it is going. Leaders must invoke an alchemy of great vision. Those leaders who do not are ultimately judged failures, even though they may be popular at the moment."[3]

Developing a Vision

John Gardner once declared that leaders "conceive and articulate goals that lift people out of their petty preoccupations, carry them above the conflicts that tear a society apart, and unite them in pursuit of objectives worthy of their best efforts."[4]

The following steps seem necessary if leaders are to conceive powerful goals, communicate them to others, and gain their people's enthusiastic acceptance.

1. Gather grass-roots input.

Those being led, and that means, for example, children in a family, students of a school, members of a parish, employees of a company, Catholics in a diocese, citizens of a community need to have ownership of the vision sketched for them. Unless they buy into the dream, it will not significantly motivate them. An effective vision such as this grows out of a usually lengthy and sometimes tedious consultation process that involves as many of the "led" as possible.

The diocese of Manchester in New Hampshire, as an illustration, launched a five-year plan during 1990. However, that visionary collection of goals, objectives, and strategies for diocesan agencies and local parishes had emerged only after several years of consultative meetings.

First, 200 representatives from throughout the state assembled for two days to assess in a prayerful, reflective way the current needs of the diocese and to express in a set of priorities their dreams about tomorrow. Then, pertinent staff personnel tried to make those hopes realistic and specific by formulating for each expressed priority a few objectives and strategies to be achieved within five years. Finally, the bishop and his associates criss-crossed the diocese "marketing" the plan.

2. Keep repeating the dream.

When Father Howard Hubbard became chief shepherd for the

diocese of Albany in New York, he was one of the youngest bishops in the country entrusted with that responsibility.

Early on he issued a pastoral letter, *We Are His People*, sharing "my vision for our Church as we journey together as a people of faith."

Some years afterward he told me that he was surprised how often the message and the dream needed to be reiterated. Printing the text in the diocesan paper, holding a media conference, convening parish leaders, and sending out copies to pastoral ministers were necessary and helpful communication steps, but not enough. He had to repeat the vision again and again.

A decade later, Bishop Hubbard reviewed the results of his original pastoral letter and set forth a new series of goals. Called "We Are God's Priestly People," the text carries a subtitle: "A Vision for the Church of Albany for the 1990s."

I presume that the now less youthful shepherd is prepared to spend much of his time and energy during these last years of the second millennium restating this vision over and over to the people of the Albany diocese.

3. *Express the vision in some captivating way.*

Warren Bennis, a professor of business administration at the University of Southern California, a former college president, and a consultant to companies as well as governments, wrote in one of his books on leaders:

"If there is a spark of genius in the leadership function at all, it must lie in this transcending ability, a kind of magic, to assemble—out of all the variety of images, signals, forecasts, and alternatives—a clearly articulated vision of the future that is at once simple, easily understood, clearly desirable, and energizing."[5]

That articulation may be only a word, a series of catchy phrases, a picture or a symbolic action. Yet it must be simple, easily understood, clearly desirable, and energizing.

• Jesse Jackson mesmerized participants and viewers of a national convention by surrounding himself with his family and urging all to "keep hope alive, keep hope alive, keep hope alive."

• Pope John Paul II gave a silent vision of forgiveness simply by visiting in a Roman prison cell the man who had shot him. That event, captured in a photo which was then instantly communicated throughout the world, spoke powerfully to millions about the need to forgive.

• The Geneseo and Wyoming Railroad is a short-line regional carrier that links the huge Retsof salt mine near Rochester, New York, with the outside world. But the company also repairs damaged and disabled, "bad order" freight cars from other railroads across the United States.

A yellow switch engine that shuttles battered cars from one shop to another has this motto printed underneath the engineer's window: "When we work as a team, we are unbeatable." Clearly someone in the organization believes that conceiving, articulating, and communicating a vision are important steps for the company's operation.

However, when I asked a trainman something specific about the railroad, he replied, "I don't know. They don't tell us nothing." Apparently the teamwork vision has broken down in practice, at least in his case, or has yet to catch on successfully. Either "they" aren't talking or perhaps he wasn't listening.

• Executives of the New York Knicks coaxed Pat Riley out of a brief retirement to coach their troubled basketball team. The sizeable salary offered surely was a factor in persuading Riley to resume an active courtside role. But the more significant motivating force seemed to be the challenge to mold a collection of what he termed talented, but underachieving athletes into a winning unit.

Riley's single-minded approach from the beginning was to stress teamwork and unselfishness, to predict that success will come if players work for each other, to make the Knicks "one, big, happy family" on and off the court.

"We're winning," says Riley. "We keep preaching, we keep believing in it, teaching each person that your success is really derived from the efforts of your teammates.

"The more you try to help them, the more you're going to get back, the more we screen for one another and feel good about each other."

The new coach has worked wonders for the Knicks and especially for guard Mark Jackson. After a stardom first year, Jackson slipped badly over the next two seasons, heard boos or catcalls from the Madison Square Garden crowds, and expected to be traded.

But his own hard work and Riley's guidance resurrected Mark Jackson. He was quick to credit his coach and praised his leadership abilities.

"We're having fun," Jackson remarked. "Guys are accepting their roles and are willing to do whatever it takes to win. It's no egos. And it starts from upstairs. It starts from coach being a leader.

"We have a great coach . . . a guy who everybody on this team believes in. That's a big difference."[6]

Although Jackson has since been traded to the Los Angeles Clippers, I would judge that his views about Riley remain the same.

A catchy phrase, a basic concept, a vision proclaimed in various ways over and over clearly caught on and made a difference.

• The nurses in one unit of a local hospital have posted in the hallway bulletin board a home-made, computerized slogan that simply states, "The Fifth floor cares."

• Symbols, alone or accompanied by a word or phrase, can be particularly effective in communicating the leader's vision. By their very nature, symbols have a mysterious power of evoking conscious or unconscious reactions within people.

For example, in the first *Rocky* film, the star, after a punishing period of training, runs up the steps at the Art Museum in Philadelphia with both fists raised high, as the sound track blasts out its victorious, triumphant melody. In some vicarious way, many audiences identified with that struggle and victory and— unusual for a movie—roared their approval.

Our ordinary and special days are filled with symbols that speak to us, like a flag or a flower, the yellow ribbons at home during Operation Desert Storm, or Christmas lights on houses throughout a neighborhood.

Effective television advertising blends verbal and visual images together in such a way that they give a message and motivate a viewer. The scene is but a few seconds long—a couple in love, the gift of a ring and "Diamonds are forever"—but sponsors hope that the image will trigger powerful responses in those who see and hear their advertisement.

True leaders not only conceive the vision but convey it through some powerful image created from a word, a phrase, a sound, a symbol—or any combination of these elements.

William Norman observed these three steps in developing AM-TRAK's marketing strategy for the 1980s. He gathered input from as many staff people as possible, combined the suggestions into a comprehensive visionary 100-point plan, and then implemented the recommendations by repeating the dream over and over again. Without realizing it, he is following today the same leadership technique in communicating a vision to his two children.

A Christian Vision

Those who preach or teach the Christian message of necessity must be visionary leaders. The fundamental truths proclaimed by Christ and taught by the church deal with an individual or a group's future. They speak about tomorrow. They hold out a vision of something still to come.

For example, the very first phrases uttered by Jesus in Mark's gospel are a call to change. "Reform your lives and believe in the gospel" (Mark 1:15). In other words, turn away from darkness and start living in the light. Change your behavior and accept the good news of a better life. Give up what is bad and become something better.

At the same time, Christ also announces, "This is the time of fulfillment. The reign of God is at hand." The gospels and other New Testament texts describe the nature of that new kingdom. It will be one of justice and peace, mercy and love. Followers of Christ are called, not only to improve their own lives but also to build this better world here on earth.

Nevertheless, both Jesus Christ and his followers keep reminding us that the fullness of the kingdom is yet to come, that our citizenship is not on this earth, that our permanent home awaits us in the life to come. The ultimate vision thus is one of life after death where there is a new heaven and a new earth, where we see God face to face and where tears are no more. In a word, the reign of God is already, but not yet.

To develop and sustain any vision, a leader needs reflective time and quiet space. We will discuss that point in the next chapter.

✦ ✦ ✦

A Quote to Ponder: "The very essence of leadership is [that] you have to have a vision. It's got to be a vision you articulate clearly and forcefully on every occasion. You can't blow an uncertain trumpet." —Theodore M. Hesburgh[7]

A Biblical Role Model: Abraham, given a command and a vision from the Lord, left his comfortable situation and immediately "went as the Lord directed him."—Genesis 12–25

2

READING AND REFLECTION

Time is the most precious commodity of all, and there never seems enough of it to do everything we want to do and need to do. The shortage of time is particularly difficult for leaders who need quiet moments in which they can pause and reflect, make plans, and look ahead. Those thoughtful pieces of time are extremely important in successful leadership.

Over the years Barbara and Francis (Dutch) Scholtz have recognized in their own lives the need for regular times of reflection. They have also developed patterns that provide them with such moments on a daily basis.

Barbara and Francis Scholtz
Married Couple, Parents, Religious Educators

It hurts to grow up with a mother who is emotionally troubled and has suffered a nervous breakdown, and with a frequently absent and unpredictable father.

The childhood of Barbara Lucas in such a dysfunctional family setting left her with permanent inner scars. But she did receive some positive gifts from these parents. The young Wisconsin girl inherited a talent and love for music from her mentally ill mother. Her father, a self-made man who was moderately successful in the workplace, provided for the family's basic material needs. Moreover, both father and mother handed down the Roman Catholic religious tradition to their daughter.

Her parents were not particularly devout, but from her earliest years Barbara found that she was strongly drawn toward prayer and spiritual realities. "I don't know why, but during Lent I would walk each morning in the dark and often bitter cold to attend Mass."

Francis Scholtz was born in 1922 and, like his future wife, he was raised in Wisconsin. He, too, inherited significant musical gifts and began piano lessons when he was in the second grade. His father and mother, very affectionate and caring parents, were also exceptionally religious people. Since they lived in a small town in which musicians were scarce, their son at age twelve became the parish organist. For the rest of his adolescent years, Francis spent many hours in the local church playing at Masses and directing the tiny church choir.

He left for college to study music, but many people urged him to become a priest. Scholtz says, "I well remember making a conscious decision that I would not be a priest because I liked girls too much. But I also promised God I would give my life to serving the church, probably because of the pressure put on me to be a priest and the guilt I felt about my decision."

The looming threat of war prompted Scholtz to drop out of college during his freshman year and enlist in the air force. After completing basic training in radio communications, he was sent to Wheeler Field at Pearl Harbor and suffered through the surprise attack by the Japanese on December 7, 1941.

"We had been on alert for three months, aware of the Japanese fleet nearby," Scholtz recalls. "But on Saturday, for no known reason, we were taken off the alertness order. Our C.O. couldn't understand it, and told us so, but let us go into town on leave for the night. It seemed strange, too, that our planes were then lined up out in the open away from their protective barriers and our weapons placed under lock and key."

Scholtz took advantage of the unexpected free evening to play at a dance in the officers' club some distance away. He

returned late to the barracks and retired. He awoke early
on that fateful morning and walked about, half-asleep and
without his glasses, wondering whether to go to early Mass
or climb back into bed for a few more hours of sleep. He
heard an explosion, looked out the door, saw a plane speed
by, and, despite his limited vision, he could make out the
red rising sun on its fuselage.

The rest of the day was filled with chaos and fear, urgent
prayer, and utter dismay.

"That was a terrible experience for Dutch," his wife observed during my conversation with them, obviously having
heard her husband describe the attack many times. "His
best friend was killed during the attack and a bullet from
one of the strafing planes brushed past his ear and embed-
ded itself in a sandbag behind him. He dug the bullet out
and kept it for a long time."

Where did the nickname "Dutch" originate?

After Pearl Harbor, Scholtz saw action on several Pacific
islands, including an extended period at Guadalcanal. Two
Jewish buddies, noting his deep religious temperament and
his close association with the Catholic chaplain, jokingly
compared him to the New York/Chicago gangster Dutch
Schultz, and labeled him "Dutch." The name stuck and has
been with Scholtz ever since.

The Guadalcanal days were difficult for Scholtz. "We went
through forty-eight consecutive nights of bombing—nui-
sance bombings. I hated the war and hated the bombings.
I couldn't wait for morning to come. I prayed, talked to
God, asking for the night soon to be over."

After four and a half years of wartime service, Dutch
returned home to the Midwest and resumed his musical
studies at Lawrence University in Appleton, Wisconsin.
Upon graduation, he went to Northwestern, and obtained
a Master's Degree in music.

During those years he met and married Barbara, who
was eight years younger than he was. He accepted a job at
St. Joseph's Church in Appleton so she could complete her
own undergraduate studies in music at Lawrence. Francis

took the position, teacher in the Catholic school and musician for the parish church, initially as a temporary measure, but continued with it for almost two decades.

Those were tough times for the Scholtzes. Barbara cared for their two small children and Dutch earned meager paychecks (typical for church employees then), putting in seventy-five-hour workweeks.

Two pivotal developments in those Appleton days changed their lives in significant ways.

First, they linked with several couples to form a Christian Family Movement unit, learning through their regular meetings how to pray in a freer, less formal fashion. At the same time, Barbara started scripture studies on a fairly regular basis. That study naturally overflowed into other aspects of her life, making their prayer together and with the group more biblically oriented. Second, despite his very meager salary, they began to tithe, giving 10 percent of their income for the church and the poor. Both the freer prayer and regular tithing were relatively uncommon practices at the time for American Catholics.

In 1968 Dutch agreed to become coordinator of education for the Diocese of Sioux Falls, South Dakota. Barbara was not pleased with the move. "I cried all the way there. I was leaving friends and going to the desert. But it turned out to be a beautiful place."

It also turned out to be a place of professional accomplishment for Dutch and of personal growth for both Scholtzes.

Dutch—in a pioneering move—made extensive use of videotapes for religious education purposes throughout that rural area of the nation. Few church educators in the United States were then taking advantage of this medium. Yet, Francis was regularly present at conferences or lectures to capture on camera the wisdom of some visiting expert or famous speaker.

During their six years at Sioux Falls the Scholtzes took an active part in several contemporary spiritual movements, including Cursillo, Marriage Encounter, and the Charismatic Renewal. They also had to work with and through their college-age son's intense religious experiences. Their son became deeply interested in an evangelical style of worship that emphasized a personal relationship to Jesus, praying and singing in tongues, heavy reliance upon the Bible, and a literal interpretation of scripture and prayer for healing. This was all quite different from the traditional Roman Catholic approach. Those combined events further altered their way of praying. For the first time the Scholtzes began to pray aloud and they became comfortable sharing their personal prayer with others. They also read or studied Scripture on a regular, serious basis. Eventually the Scholtzes adopted a practice of starting each day together with thirty minutes of prayerful reflection and spiritual reading.

Church leaders in Minnesota's Twin Cities, learning about Dutch's imaginative talents and proven successes, hired him in 1974 as the director of education for the Archdiocese of St. Paul. This was a quantum leap; he moved from his post as coordinator of a relatively small diocesan operation to the supervisor of an archdiocesan office responsible for 39,000 Catholic school students and 90,000 public school pupils receiving religious education.

Scholtz soon integrated his spiritual, reflective style into staff operating procedures. There were daily opportunities for prayer at work. Also, every Wednesday at 8:30 A.M. he arranged a Mass or a prayer service for all Catholic Education employees. Afterward staff members gathered for coffee, doughnuts, and thirty minutes of informal conversations, followed by a formal staff meeting. Moreover, twice each year personnel gathered at some retreat center away from the office for a day of meditative pondering. That emphasis produced results. Employees often remarked about the peaceful atmosphere prevalent in this setting, a quality Scholtz attributes to his encouragement of moments for reflection.

During the 1980s, Barbara and Dutch became actively involved in promoting tithing under a specific process called sacrificial giving. They had been practicing this form of contributing to the church for twenty years. They now began to speak nationally about its value both for the individual giver and for the parish church. That brought them ultimately, in 1986, to Jacksonville, ꟻlorida, when Dutch was hired as the first director of stewardship for the diocese of St. Augustine. Barbara started at the same time to coordinate from their home more than 100 volunteer speakers from across the country, who travel about the United States, mostly on weekends, visiting Catholic churches to convey the message of sacrificial giving or tithing.

The Scholtzes continue to begin each day together with those thirty minutes of silent prayer, biblical readings, and shared reflections. Dutch has likewise continued to weave his prayerful approach into office procedures. Both Scholtzes are continuing to make separate annual retreats, stepping aside for several days, in some quiet setting, to rest a while, pray, and ponder.

The Scholtzes' two children are grown now and have given them a half dozen grandchildren. Their son is a college professor of English and their daughter is a symphony musician. The Scholtz children have taken somewhat different directions in faith and practice from their parents. This concerns the Scholtzes, but Barbara comments, "We want our kids to know that we love them regardless. They know what we believe. Now, as they have their own children, they express their gratitude for what we did for them as parents. They never had done this before, and it is really nice to hear it. They also tell us that even though we were not able to take big trips because of our modest income, they never felt deprived."

The Scholtzes' pattern of set aside daily time for reading and reflection has borne dividends in their personal lives, in their professional careers, and, obviously, in their parenting roles.[1]

A Busy, But Reflective Bishop

Albert Ottenweller looks, at 6ft. 5in., like a former college basketball player. And so he was, for two years, before he began his seminary studies at Catholic University in Washington. Today, almost a half century later, the lanky man has just retired after serving for fifteen years as bishop of the Steubenville, Ohio, diocese.

Bishop Ottenweller talks and acts in visionary terms. During his earlier days as pastor of two large (2000 family) parishes in the Toledo area, he developed a host of creative programs. They included the division of the church into small districts, formation of lay leaders for each section, birth preparation classes, and communication skill-building sessions for couples who were married less than a decade. As shepherd of Steubenville, he continued this type of leadership that looks beyond the present and imagines what might become in the future.

Both that vision of tomorrow and the strength to pursue his dreams came from a daily period of prayer early in the morning. He offered Mass at 7:00 A.M. with a group of religious brothers next door to his home. He then ate breakfast, and afterward prayed privately for an hour or so. The bishop found that these moments alone with God not only provided answers to the enormously difficult challenges that faced him, but also brought him great peace and joy.

Making Major Decisions

Bishop Ottenweller is far from alone in his discovery of the crucial importance of a little solitude for creativity. Contemporary secular business executives and religious pastoral leaders have made this identical discovery: Time for reading and reflection is crucial for their personal well-being and their professional effectiveness.

Many management experts maintain that a primary function of executives is to make major decisions. Those judgments require that the decision maker step aside for a substantial undisturbed period to study the available data and to ponder all possibilities. Then the leader decides and subsequently communicates the decisions to all individuals who will be affected by her or his decision.

Those mentors recommend that even, or perhaps especially, the most harried executive remains home one morning a week to carry out this essential decision-making task. Once they arrive at the office, busywork, telephone calls, and staff interruptions derail the reflective process and lead to great frustration.

My uncle George arranged for that necessary quiet time in a different way. For over four decades he managed a busy district office for the General Motors Acceptance Corporation. Throughout those many years, Uncle George regularly arrived at the office about an hour before anyone else came to work. During these sixty minutes he was able, in a calm and serene atmosphere, to read memoranda, sift through suggestions, and arrive at needed major decisions. Then the secretaries arrived, the phones began to ring, the first mail reached his desk, and staff members appeared at his office seeking decisions on various matters.

Parish priests and pastoral leaders would concur with the experiences of the Steubenville bishop and these business executives. They know the futility of trying to prepare a homily, outline a class, or detail a presentation while at their office desks.

In that situation people frequently either call or come in unexpectedly with very legitimate concerns. We respond to them, but with our minds remaining back at the homily, class, or talk. Our attention is divided and afterward we generally feel guilty or regretful that the caller or visitor may have hung up or gone away sensing our distracted attentiveness. We then experience a double negative. The sermon or lecture has not been completed; yet appropriate care was not given to the person claiming our attention.

The only resolution of this dilemma is to allocate on a regular basis some quiet time and an away place for prayer, reading, reflection, creative writing, and major decision making.

A Place Away

In the midst of writing this chapter I faced a difficult two-week challenge serving as pastor of our 1500 family parish. A New York State agency working with developmentally disabled adults was seeking to establish an additional "Group Home" in a section of our Camillus township. Several local property owners, not unexpectedly, objected strongly to the establishment of the home in their neighborhood.

In view of this bitter opposition we felt compelled to support the state's efforts not only because of obvious Christian principles but also because of specific personal concerns—three of the disabled residents who would live in this new home were regular parishioners at our church. We knew them, cared for them, and had involved them actively in the life of the parish.

Our supportive measures included the preparation of an informational flier for insertion in the Sunday church bulletin. To compose this four-page document, I had to leave the rectory office, drive to my cottage hideaway, work in seclusion for several hours, and then return to the church with the draft text. Trying to accomplish this at a desk in the busy rectory would have been an exercise in futility.

Not everyone, of course, has a cottage by some lake, a camp in the woods, a room away from crowds, or a house separate from work. But with some ingenuity it is possible to discover an easily accessible quiet space somewhere, a location suitable for the type of reading and reflection that leadership people need. First, however, the leader must recognize the importance of, or better, the essential value of such a spot.

As we see later, and as Dutch Scholtz did in the Twin Cities, staff personnel and leadership people of a parish or organization benefit from a full "retreat" day away from the office once or twice a year. These help keep one's vision alive and/or facilitate the development of a new vision.

It is also clear that leaders profit from a more extended, sabbatical-style break from their responsibilities.

A Time Away

In 1990, graduate number 1000 passed through the portals of St. Patrick's Seminary at Menlo Park, California.

Were they young men ready for ordination to the priesthood? No. Rather they were veteran priests—average age around fifty—who had just completed a three-month renewal program at the Vatican II Institute for Clergy Formation located in a building on the grounds of that institution south of San Francisco.

Every fall and midwinter over the past two decades, three dozen priests from both within the United States and from beyond our borders have assembled at St. Patrick's for one of those institutes. A roughly equal mix of diocesan clergy and religious order priests, they represent a great range of ministries. Some are parish priests, others are foreign missionaries; some teach in Catholic schools, others serve as hospital chaplains; some work in church administration, others act as retreat directors. During the span of their stay at Menlo Park, these men enjoy exceptional opportunities that are designed to renew them intellectually, mentally, physically, and spiritually.

Five days each week they gather in a lecture room setting for two-hour morning and evening sessions. Distinguished outside speakers address them on various theological and pastoral topics. The list of professors is impressive, with nationally known experts appearing for several days or week-long seminars.

Participants take psychological tests and learn how the Myers-Briggs personality profile or Enneagram analysis can help them in their pastoral ministry after they leave Vatican II. Professional therapeutic counselors are available for each one who wishes such assistance.

The men weigh in at the beginning and weigh out at the end. They are encouraged to develop a regular pattern of physical exercise, learn the value of healthy eating habits and, in general, recover an awareness probably learned years earlier that a sound body and a sound mind go together.

They can pray the Liturgy of the Hours regularly in community if they so desire. These men likewise celebrate the Eucharist daily either with the seminary's student body, or together as a whole group, or in their own small subunits. Each member of the institute has a spiritual director; the members make an extended retreat during the session; the participants regularly visit parishes of the area to experience liturgical celebrations in different settings.

There are days and clusters of days off, giving the participants opportunities to visit and witness the sights and sounds of the Bay area as well as to travel to other points of interest on the West

Coast. During these three months there is also the immeasurable growth that happens through the mere interchange among priests of such diverse backgrounds.

Does it work? Do the graduates leave renewed?

One man, a pastor for some twenty years, told me he came to Menlo Park broken and afflicted with every symptom of "burnout." He was angry and depressed (they are connected), tired, discouraged, bitter, and devoid of all enthusiasm. His anger is gone now; he feels rested; the man senses that a real positive change in attitude has occurred within him.

Bishop Joseph Hart of Cheyenne, Wyoming, was the first bishop of a United States diocese to enroll at the Vatican II Institute. He praises the process and judges that it has been a wonderful renewal for him in every way. The exposure to so many ideas in the company of fine priests has expanded his vision and "tickled my imagination."

Leaders need to take such time away.

Sacred and Secular Benefits

Christian leaders find that some daily moments away in a quiet place are necessary not only for developing a vision or making a decision but for connecting with God through prayer. In this they can follow the example of well-known and successful teachers, preachers, and healers from every age who have found time and space for personal prayer each day.

• Jesus, of course, would be their model. The four gospels note at least several dozen occasions in which Christ was at prayer or went off to pray or spent time praying.[2] For example, after curing many who were variously afflicted, he rose early the next morning, went off to a lonely place in the desert, and "there he was absorbed in prayer" (Mark 1:35). Jesus also once departed to a mountain, "spent the night in prayer to God," then came down and made a major decision—he selected the Twelve, the apostles, the future leaders of his church (Luke 6:12–16).

• Christ also taught these Twelve that they should find time and space away from their everyday work. Early on, these leaders returned flushed with the success of their preaching and healing efforts. Their master responded with, "Come away by yourselves to a deserted place and rest a while" (Mark 6:30–33).

• Centuries later, St. Francis observed a similar pattern. He traveled continually and preached energetically, but regularly returned to Assisi and withdrew to an isolated wilderness by himself for a lengthy period of prayer and reflection.

• During our contemporary period, *The Cross and The Switchblade* author/minister David Wilkerson, Archbishop Fulton J. Sheen, Mother Teresa of Calcutta, and writer/lecturer Henri Nouwen—all set aside daily substantial periods for prayer and reflection.

• Stephan Kovalski became a priest in France to work with the poor and for justice. Eventually he made his way to India and secured church permission to live and work in a section of abject poverty within Calcutta, a locale called by him the City of Joy.

He describes the hardships of his first day as an isolated stranger in that impoverished area and how his habit of prayer helped him.

"God only knows how alone I felt that first morning!" he was to say. "Not being able to breathe a single word of the languages spoken in the slum, it was like being deaf and dumb. And not being able to lay my hands on a little wine, I was deprived even of the comfort of being able to celebrate the Eucharist in the darkness of my den. Fortunately, there was still prayer!"

Prayer! For years Stephan Kovalski had begun each day with an hour's contemplation. Whether he was in a plane, a train, or a roomful of immigrant workmen, he emptied himself, turned to God, gave himself up to him to receive his word, or simply to say to his Creator, "Here I am, at your disposal." He also liked to open the Gospels at random and pick out a sentence such as, "Save me; or I perish," or "Salvation is of the Lord," or "In Thy presence is fullness of joy." He would study every word and every syllable turning them over in every possible direction. "It's a spiritual exercise that helps me to achieve silence," he would explain, "to find emptiness in God. If God has time to listen to me, then inevitably he has time to love me."[3]

In addition to these sacred or spiritual, prayerful or religious benefits gained by taking time away for reading and reflection, there are several secular, purely natural, or totally human benefits from this practice as well. We have mentioned conceiving and sustaining a vision as a primary one. Reducing inner stress and maintaining personal peace are others.

A study by Harvard cardiologist Herbert Benson revealed that people who practice some form of meditation once or twice a day experience a perceptible reduction in the signs of stress.[4] The Green Berets have been taught meditation techniques to make them comfortable within themselves at a deep inner level. They can then spend long hours hidden in enemy territory without making mental mistakes and giving away their positions.[5]

Most of us have experienced the fresh approaches, the new ideas, and the renewed enthusiasms we experience after an extended, restful, and satisfying vacation. Our batteries are recharged, the creative juices begin to flow again, and we are eager once more to launch out on challenging projects.

During those times for reading and reflection we usually sort out and may even establish certain priorities in our personal and professional lives—the subject of the next chapter.

A Quote to Ponder: "Those who do not set aside a certain place and time each day to do nothing else but pray can never expect their unceasing thought to become unceasing prayer."—Henri Nouwen[6]

A Biblical Role Model: Jesus, who went about doing good, often retired to deserted places and prayed.—Luke 5:12–16

3

PRIORITIES

Time is not the only limited resource in our lives. Money, energy, staff, equipment, opportunity itself may each or all be in short supply. Leaders know this, and they establish and follow priorities that let them make the best use of the resources they have. And setting wise priorities also helps all of us keep our lives clearly focused—and at least somewhat peaceful.

In her relatively young life, the woman described in the following vignette has had to confront the harsh realities of limited resources, and she has made some hard priority decisions to get the most out of her resources.

Susan Champlin Taylor
Wife, Mother, Senior Editor of **Modern Maturity**

Being the child of a famous parent or parents can be troublesome for some offspring. Apparently that is not so for Susan Champlin Taylor. Her father (my brother) has been, during most of her life, a well-known Los Angeles film critic, television host, and newspaper editor. Did this create a problem?

"Not at all," Susan said to me. "Someone remarked to my older brother that it must be tough always living in the shadow of a famous father. He quickly replied that it's not a shadow, it's more of a glow. I found it has always been great. My dad is so well loved and respected that whenever

I am introduced as his daughter, people brighten up and seem very pleased to meet me."

Susan was born in 1961, attended Catholic grammar and high schools in Los Angeles, and then moved on to Stanford for college. There she majored in English, graduating with Phi Beta Kappa honors. But Susan's love for language and writing started much earlier in the home, mostly from her father, but also from her mother who holds a doctorate in the history of science.

"Even though my dad was very busy during my growing-up years and mom was the one who related to us more on a day-to-day basis," Susan remarked as she held her weeks-old, firstborn child, "all of us absorbed a love for words from both of them. Puns were always flying around the dinner table and they regularly corrected our grammar."

While Susan's parents deepened her love for words and sharpened her writing skills, they provided this bright young woman with an even greater gift—unconditional care and support.

"They always supported me in whatever I had or wanted to do. They just loved me. It didn't matter what I wanted to do or become. I never felt any pressure from my parents to go here or do that. In high school I loved being an actress and wanted to become one. They supported that. Later I gave this idea up and turned to writing. They supported that. And at Stanford when I felt a need for 'stopping out,' taking a quarter off to find out some things about myself, they supported that."

During that quarter of "stopping out" in the spring of her sophomore year, Susan came home, worked for Disney Studios and sorted through her own priorities—why am I in school and what do I really want to be. By the end, she had clarified things for herself. She decided to finish college and obtain a degree. Always a good student, it was relatively easy for her to make up the necessary units. Moreover, upon return in the fall Susan went to England and studied there as part of a Stanford studies abroad program.

After graduation Susan was at loose ends about what to do, knowing only that she wanted to work with words. At the suggestion of her father, who had been a writer at *Time* and *Life* magazines before he joined the *Los Angeles Times* as entertainment editor, Susan sent a résumé to the Los Angeles bureau chief of *People* magazine. Susan was hired as a reporter. The good timing was a piece of luck, but as the famous director Billy Wilder likes to say, luck favors the well prepared. Susan did a writing stint at the magazine's main office in New York and had a lively time in Los Angeles covering cat shows and beautiful baby contests. But she was not heartbroken when the magazine reduced its staff and she was let go. It was time for her to move on.

After a year of free-lance writing, Susan answered a blind ad in the *Los Angeles Times*. The American Association of Retired Persons was looking for an associate editor for its publication, *Modern Maturity*. The AARP liked Susan's credentials, hired her, and quite rapidly advanced her to a promotion as one of the magazine's senior editors.

In the midst of all these career shifts, Susan at age twenty-three in 1984 married her long-time boyfriend, Stephen Taylor, who was also a Stanford graduate. Did she experience any tensions over the mix of marriage and career?

"There was never a problem with this, Uncle Joe. Steve has always been a strong supporter of my career. He supported me during the tough days when I was unemployed. He was thrilled when I got the job with *Modern Maturity*. But time has sometimes been a problem for us. For two years after our marriage we both were working full time and Steve was also studying for his Master's in Engineering at UCLA. He was often away much of the time on weekends. We had only fleeting hours for each other. That was hard and there were times I resented this."

What about children?

"We always wanted to have children, but felt a need to discover the right time, a time when our careers were established and we could buy a suitable house. We were living in a troublesome neighborhood where you hesitated to go out by yourself. We were not comfortable bringing up a baby there. We wanted a nicer section in which to live.

"We saved for years," Susan commented, tiny Annie Meredith Margaret Taylor sleeping on her lap. "We never went wild on things. We did take two trips to Europe, and had good vacations, but our cars are eleven years old. We didn't buy luxuries and seldom went out for dinner. We made a conscious decision to save for the house. Steve is great on budgets and we followed a tight, lean one. We finally bought a beautiful home in July and don't anticipate moving for many years. By December we were expecting."

Annie arrived on August 8, three and a half weeks early, by cesarean section. She has brought great joy to her parents, but has also understandably taxed their time and energy reserves.

"I am nursing Annie, which takes a lot of time. It may be 9:00 in the evening and Steve and I haven't eaten supper yet. Annie doesn't sleep through the night yet, so Steve and I are both tired. And we don't have as much time to focus on each other as before, so sometimes I am a little sad about that.

"But at the same time, everything else in life now seems sort of unimportant," Susan notes. "There is nothing more amazing than this child. I talk to people at work about how things are there, but right now I don't really care.

"I could stare at Annie for hours and simply watch her breathe or make faces.

"It's scary, too. We feel so totally responsible. She can't do anything for herself yet. What if I mess up, do something wrong?"

How will Susan balance being a mother and editing at *Modern Maturity?*

"I am going back to work. I can't afford not to because of the large house payments. But I won't be returning until January. *Modern Maturity* lets me do that with its six months' leave policy.

"I have mixed feelings about going back to work. I love my job, but now, knowing my feelings for Annie, it is going to be so hard to leave her. Even if there is a good day-care setting for her, I will probably be crying in the ladies' room or at my desk.

"That is the downside of owning such a nice house. It would be ideal to have the choice of being a full-time mom."

Susan has a double leadership role now. She is daily in

countless ways touching Annie's future. But she also has and will touch many as a writer/editor for the AARP publication, a magazine with the largest (22 million) circulation in the United States.

"It can be devastating to think of that huge readership—what if I make a mistake? But on the other hand, it is equally rewarding to think about the consequences if I do something good for others.

"When my article 'A Thoughtful Word, A Healing Touch' appeared—which you helped me with—a lot of people wrote for permission to reprint the piece. They said it would be helpful for visitors to hospitals and for church people, that it was really beautiful. I was proud of that.

"The cover story I did on children at risk in America painted a grim picture of youngsters growing up in poverty, but it also talked about possible solutions. I felt it was influential and exerted a positive impact."

Susan Champlin Taylor has in but three decades on earth found it necessary on several occasions to sort out the currents in her life and establish some basic personal priorities. She has likewise discovered that time, money, and energy are limited resources. We have only so much, and not usually enough of these three elements. That fact, too, requires establishing priorities and carrying them out.[1]

Limited Resources

• For a century or more, a train daily shuttled carloads of broken limestone perhaps twenty miles down from the Jamesville, New York, quarry to the sprawling Solvay Process plant. There about 1600 workers transformed by special procedures the crushed rock into valuable chemicals for distribution here and abroad.

But times changed, methods shifted, and what was once a very successful operation for the Solvay company now had become a losing venture, or, at best, a marginally profitable business. Corporate leaders of the current owner—Allied Chemical—thus decided several years ago at its New Jersey offices to close the plant down and dismantle the buildings. The company could earn a greater profit on their investment at other locations. It would reap a better return on its money elsewhere.

These people recognize, as does my niece Susan, that there is only a limited amount of financial and material resources in this world. Their goal is to maximize the return by making the most effective use of what they have.

• Headlines in the secular press a few years back announced the closing or consolidating of churches, schools, institutions, and offices in the archdiocese of Chicago. The reasons were lack of funds, a huge financial deficit, and a red bottom line budget. Leaders closed or consolidated these churches, schools, institutions, and offices not because they were ineffective, wasteful, or superfluous. They were not trimming fat from the budget or eliminating useless positions. All of these people and agencies were pursuing good goals and accomplishing worthwhile tasks.[2]

But the money was not there. Something had to give. Leadership people, in an always painful move, needed to decide how they could best use the limited dollars that were available. Those who were cut back or out may have been doing well, but others could do better. If there were ample funds, no reductions or eliminations would have occurred. But since that was not the case, the leaders who were responsible had to make a judgment about the optimum use of the monies on hand. Their problem was how to achieve the greatest good for the greatest number in the archdiocese of Chicago.

• In these well-publicized days of a clergy shortage within the Catholic Church throughout most of the United States, a particular bishop faces a difficult decision. He ordains one or only a few new priests. To what type of ministry will he direct these freshly ordained men? Will they be assigned as parish priests, teachers in schools, chaplains for hospitals, or college campus ministers? All are important, necessary functions. But there are not enough clergy to go around, to fill these slots. Again, the bishop with his advisers must make some type of a priority judgment.

• If secular corporations and church organizations must cope with limited resources and best deal with this challenge through a priority-making decision process, so, too, must we as individuals in our personal lives. There is simply not enough time every day to accomplish all that most of us would like to do or judge that we should do. No one's supply of energy is inexhaustible. Few people are so financially secure that money matters never concern them.

Susan has had to work through this priority-making scenario several times already in her young life. She had to decide her real goal or purpose in college; she and Steve had to work through the tensions of too little time for each other during the first years of their married life as she developed her career and he pursued his degree; they both made the purchase of a suitable house in a decent neighborhood a financial priority for them as they budgeted their funds; both have experienced the great blessing and heavy burden of a baby in their midst with the consequent drain upon their time, energies, and finances. Susan is now struggling to balance a career, motherhood, and a spousal relationship.

Learning how to establish priorities is thus crucial for corporations and churches, for family units and individual persons—in fact for everyone and every group in today's world.

Establishing Priorities

There are two indispensable steps in the priority-making decision process, especially for those in positions of service to others, such as parents, clergy, health care personnel, teachers, and social workers: the ability to say no and a skill for responding to crisis situations.

1. *The ability to say no.*
It is not bad to be a fixer, a savior, or a helper. Supplying food or providing clothes, listening to another's trouble or healing broken bones, standing by a friend in grief or assisting a colleague with decisions are simply contemporary examples of Christian behavior. Jesus' famous words apply: "Whatever you do (or do not do) to one of these the least of my brothers or sisters, that you do (or do not do) to me" (Matthew 25:31–46).

But we sometimes slip into a trap and find that we *need* to be the fixer, savior, or helper more than the other needs or wants to be fixed, saved, or helped. Moreover, we may discover that we are starting to see ourselves as *the* fixer, savior, helper of all people, at all times, in all circumstances.

There are usually certain warning signals or noticeable symptoms of this unhealthy development within us. We grow quite intense about the person or situation; our energy level is far above or out of proportion to the circumstance confronting us; we seem obsessed with the matter; we lose our focus and our peace; we take ourselves too seriously and judge ourselves indispensable for any solution.

People who have slipped into that state obviously will find it difficult, nearly impossible to say no to any request. But others in the helping professions who have maintained a better balance nevertheless can find it hard to respond negatively when someone asks for help of some sort. They see someone truly hurting or a situation crying out for a solution. Their hearts are touched and they wish to fix, save, or help.

Still, no one can respond to everyone on every occasion. There must be some boundaries. Individual helpers or fixers have need of regular time and space for themselves or they will eventually discover that their own reservoirs of energy are empty. With that comes discouragement and a lack of enthusiasm, bitterness, and even some cynicism.

Those in the helping profession know by sad experience that unless they erect some personal barriers and protective boundaries this will happen. The key is the ability to say no in those circumstances when a no is necessary.

Mother Teresa of Calcutta is a model here. She surely was and is dedicated to the poorest of the poor; she has given herself unsparingly to those who are hurting. But she insists that her sisters have an hour of prayer in the morning and evening away from their work. She says, "It is not how much we do, but how much love we put into the doing" that counts.[3] When she was asked her reactions to the endless number of people that she sees who are dying or abandoned, Mother Teresa remarks, "I only do what I can do."

2. *A skill for responding to "crisis" situations.*

By the word *crisis* I do not mean suicidal or similarly desperate circumstances. Rather, I am referring to a "turning point" occasion in someone's life, a movement normally filled with considerable energy or anxiety. People in that situation call or contact someone and seek answers or assistance.

Those of us in the helping or serving professions are constantly bombarded with calls or visits of this nature. They often occur unexpectedly, and at moments when we are busy with other important matters. The task is to respond in a way that maintains our own serenity and preserves our own priorities, while extending a gracious reception and providing a certain relief for the anxious caller or visitor.

For example, about once a month someone telephones the rectory in the middle of a Saturday night to inquire about the schedule for Sunday morning Masses. That type of call is objectively unreasonable and ridiculous, but a high degree of energy and tension runs underneath the inquirer's request. They may be visitors who suddenly realize that the next day is Sunday and are anxious to arrange their schedule so they can catch a Mass. An answering machine generally resolves that problem. However, if we forget to turn it on, the temptation for the abruptly awakened clergy is to reply with a sarcastic or annoyed remark. That does not help the situation, however thoughtless the call.

Engaged couples who contact the church to arrange for their weddings are another illustration. In most cases, they are excited and elated, but also a bit nervous and concerned. They sometimes just appear at the office door, presuming that the clergy has been waiting for their unexpected arrival. Pressed with a tight schedule, the clergy person may understandably, but regrettably, respond rather curtly to the dreamy-eyed pair who then feel hurt by this lack of warmth and interest.

During a communications course at Rome, Italy, in the fall of 1976, I learned some valuable techniques for responding to these and other similar "crisis" moments.

For the Unexpected Visitor

People in "crisis" situations feel pressure to have a problem solved, a question answered, or a date reserved. That inner turmoil pushes them to take action immediately and thus to be free of their anxiety. It also causes them to ignore or forget that the person they are seeking at a church, school, or office has other obligations and other people with whom they are working. The "crisis" callers consequently show up at the door without an appointment and expect instant attention.

Responders need, first of all, to recognize the importance of the exchange and the anxiousness of the callers. That means a warm and cordial greeting to them, despite the pressures of time and schedule responders may be feeling themselves.

After greeting and seating the callers, responders then need to establish a contract before opening up the discussion. "I am delighted you are here. I wasn't expecting you and have another obligation at this moment. But I can give you five minutes right now. If we can't take care of what is on your mind in that time, I would be happy to make a later appointment when we can visit at leisure."

An engaged couple, for instance, will probably at that point blurt out their desire to arrange a wedding; the clergy person can react positively, then set up an appointment in the near future and shortly afterward send them on their way. The callers usually leave both relieved and pleased with their "crisis" resolved. The responder has dealt well, but briefly, with a potentially stress-causing interruption, and can move on to other obligations with minimal delay.

Establishing a contract at the very outset is the key to dealing with unexpected visitors.

For the Interrupting Phone Call

Most of us have had the experience of visiting in an office with someone who accepts a phone call and then talks at length with the caller. We tend to react inwardly with a variety of negative feelings during such an interruption.

The initial step in avoiding these circumstances is a clear office policy: no interruptions of personal counseling sessions except for emergencies. But even with such an established procedure, interruptions will occur, particularly by the telephone.

In those cases, we make a mental note of what the personal visitor said just prior to the interruption, excuse ourselves and deal with the phone call swiftly. "Good to talk with you, Mary. I have someone with me right now. Can we take care of the matter in a minute or can I call you back?"

After taking care of the matter or noting her phone number for a later call back, we return to the visitor and say, "You were saying that. . . ." repeating the point of the conversation before the phone interruption.

For the "Along-the-Way" Inquirer

Public persons, like the clergy, frequently are stopped on the street or in similar locations by individuals with a "Could I ask you something or talk to you for a moment?" The clergy may be greeting the rush of worshipers leaving Sunday service or heading for the hospital and thus feel torn by the single inquirer and the other responsibilities.

A contract at the outset is again the central step in managing this dilemma well. "Actually I am on my way to the hospital, but I can give you two minutes right now. If we can't clear up the matter by that time, I would be very happy to make an appointment a little later when we can visit at length."

Often the matter can be cared for in the two minutes. But, if not, the inquirer will feel satisfied with the treatment and the responder can carry on without undue delay, a delay that could otherwise create stress and tension.

As people committed to serving others, leaders will never be free of persons who arrive unexpectedly, of interrupting phone calls, and of on-the-spot inquirers. I have employed these techniques for over fifteen years and find them very liberating—they provide temporary or permanent relief for the person in "crisis," but leave me feeling satisfied that I have dealt well with a situation and yet been able to maintain a reasonable schedule of other duties.

What of those 1:30 or 4:15 Sunday morning phone calls about the Mass schedule? Make sure that the answering machine with a recorded message giving that information is turned on before you turn in.

Personal Priorities

Once leaders have recognized the need to establish priorities with regard to time, money, and energy; have learned to say no on occasion; and have developed a certain skill in managing "crisis" moments, what are some personal priorities for them? We start with a given—there are only twenty-four hours in every day. Can we distribute that time wisely? Are certain elements absolutely essential in the everyday life of effective leaders? Before prioritizing the time they have for their professional careers, should they be prioritizing the time they have for their personal lives?

The answer is yes to all those questions. The following are five suggested personal priorities:

1. *Reflection.* In the previous chapter, I discussed the importance of a leader's allocating significant time periods for study and reflection leading to major decisions. I also pointed out the value of substantive prayer moments for Christian leaders and noted the natural, stress-reducing power of meditation once or twice a day.

Carving five or ten minutes or an hour each day out of the twenty-four available for reflection (and prayer) is the first and top priority for many leadership people.

2. *Rest.* A *Time* magazine cover story, "The Sleep Gap" tells it all. Subheadings for the article read this way: "Too much to do, too little rest;" "For millions of people caught in the nation's twenty-four-hour whirl, sleep is the last thing on their mind. It shouldn't be. Lack of rest is leading to everything from poor grades to industrial accidents."[4]

Most of us know from personal experience how a lack of adequate sleep negatively impacts our attitudes, feelings, and behavior. We make molehill problems into mountainous obstacles; we find ourselves too swiftly and without basis feeling very discouraged, overwhelmed, or downcast. We react sharply to anything or anyone crossing us; we can't seem to think, speak, write, or work in our customary fashion or at our usual pace. We make bad judgments and poor choices.

How much sleep do we need? The *Time* essay maintains that

the amount of rest we require depends largely on our heredity and age. Most adults, the article reports, need about eight hours of sleep. Only 10 percent require significantly more or less sleep.[5]

As they move through adulthood, people tend to discover how much sleep they ordinarily require. At sixty plus years I know that six hours of rest is generally sufficient for me. If I dip below that, I will pay a price the next day, suffering some of the ill effects noted previously. However, I nap every midday for 10 to 20 minutes. And if I am unable to fit that horizontal break into my schedule, I will feel on edge, pressing, inefficient, and not at my best. Moreover, on other occasions, like Sunday afternoons following nonstop efforts in church that day from 6:30 A.M. to 2:30 P.M., my nap will be harder and longer. Our bodies do speak clearly to us, if we will listen.

The ability to drop off into a sound sleep within seconds and awake refreshed a dozen minutes later is a great blessing. But the ease with which I can fall asleep can be a burden as well. My friends recognize telltale signs of fatigue—the drooping eyelids at the end of a meal. Parishioners may smile knowingly when—despite his heroic struggle—the pastor's eyes close or his head nods while another priest (or even a bishop) preaches.

3. *Recreation.* This personal priority has to do with a proper amount of physical exercise each week.

The relationship of a regular physical exercise program to one's bodily, emotional, intellectual, and spiritual well-being has been so well documented and widely proclaimed that the point hardly needs to be treated.

A University of Massachusetts medical school professor states, "One of the worst things you can do is to be inactive. Moderate health activity is a health benefit. Inactivity is hazardous to your health."[6]

A scholar at the Aerobics Center in Dallas adds, "An important message to the public is that exercise is a good health habit."[7]

A Stanford professor concludes about the effects of exercise: "You feel better, you look better, you function better and you last longer."[8]

A study of American Catholic priests and their health habits revealed that those who are most healthy follow a pattern of living which includes these elements: Vacation two weeks plus every year, weekly day off and more, untroubled sleep, and exercise very often.[9] The same report, however, indicates that the frequency of exercise declines with advancing years.[10]

The American bishops, recognizing the validity of these points, have tried to remind priests of the importance of physical exercise for a healthy, vital ministry. They also encourage those studying for the priesthood to develop an appreciation of physical health and the importance of regular exercise.[11]

After running a marathon in Ottawa, Canada, ten years ago, I concluded that for me an hour of exercise five days a week should be a real priority in my life. Running, swimming, or playing handball for that period of time each week helps me physically, spiritually, emotionally, and intellectually. An annual complete medical checkup has proven the worth of such a program for my physical well-being. I may not, and usually do not, work those five times into my week—generally it comes closer to two to four occasions weekly—but regular exercise continues to be a definite priority for me.

4. *Reading*. Unless we steadily feed our mind and hearts with new ideas, our vision loses clarity and freshness and our enthusiasm wanes. A daily pattern of reading ensures this consistent nourishing of our inner selves.

My stepfather was a voracious and rapid reader. A table in our rural home contained stacks of the some forty diverse journals to which he subscribed, from *Business Week* and *Fortune* to the *New Yorker* and *Time*. Sundays always meant for him a ten-mile drive to Camden for his reserved copy of the thick *New York Times*. He was continually reading contemporary books on business, history, politics, and leadership. One never forgets that kind of impressive example.

I worked and resided in Washington for three years with Monsignor George Higgins, the nationally known labor-management expert. An avid reader and book reviewer himself, Higgins once said to me, "If anyone reads consistently two hours a day, that person will become a very well-educated individual."

Although the importance of regular reading holds true for leaders in the secular world, the practice is especially crucial for those who are serious about their spiritual growth or who hold positions of leadership in any church.

My own daily pattern is less ambitious than that espoused by Monsignor Higgins. I read a chapter of the Old Testament in the morning, a few minutes of spiritual reading at night before retiring, and professional books and magazines as time and situations allow and demand.

But Higgins is right; consistency makes the difference. If one perseveres with that daily approach, even for a few minutes each day, the amount of material one can cover will be surprising.

I am already on my second trip through the entire Old Testament just by keeping to that chapter-by-chapter daily schedule. That may not seem like much of an accomplishment to some, but it has been a source of considerable satisfaction to me. I can also cite ten books of length and more than a dozen volumes of a biblical commentary covered over the years by my few minutes every night approach.

5. *Rejuvenation.* "All work and no play makes Johnny a dull boy"—words of earthy wisdom handed down from the past. Similarly, unless leaders take time for literary and cultural pursuits, they will suffer in their ability to motivate people. Each day or at least often there must be time to relax, play, and rejuvenate. Going to the movies or the theater, watching television or scanning magazines, listening to music or attending a concert, reading poetry or devouring novels—these not only bring relaxation but also develop our imaginative and creative abilities.

Contemporary studies about the left brain–right brain experience of communication highlight this need for fostering the poetic, cultural, and artistic aspect of our lives. The left brain loves order and logic; the right brain responds to stories and images. Leaders need to touch both the left brains and the right brains of the people they lead. Regular time for rejuvenation helps us grow in our ability to move people by appealing to their right brain antennae. These are not wasted hours, but indispensable moments that deserve a priority rating in our personal allocation of the day's twenty-four hours.

Professional Priorities

The very fact that we begin the division of a day by setting aside time for these five personal priorities is in itself a priority decision. It means that we must initially take care of ourselves before we can take care of others. It means that our personal lives must take precedence over our professional lives. It means that our being or who we are is more important than our work or what we do.

Having established that priority and cut out of the twenty-four hours a significant piece to care for these five "Rs" of our personal lives described previously, how do we use a parallel approach to the remaining hours for our professional lives or efforts in the workplace?

Much of our professional priorities will be dictated by the general priorities employers set for a company or institution. But even in this framework, leaders will need processes for constantly evaluating how their limited time, energy, and financial resources are being utilized.

That will mean leaders periodically asking their secretaries to evaluate them. "How can I do things better, more effectively? Any suggestions for me? How am I wasting your time?" That will mean leaders convening staffs annually or semiannually to review, and then renew or revise their priorities.

That will mean companies or institutions constantly monitoring their short- and long-term goals and, as circumstances dictate, devising new ones.

When I first began my term as a new pastor, I arrived with a series of preconceived pastoral priorities. These were based on my years in the priestly ministry, my lectures around the nation, and my study of church matters. These were subject to change after learning more about the particular needs of parishioners. However, they provided a framework within which to launch my efforts and to allocate my time, energy, and finances.

These pastoral priorities were Sunday worship and preaching, daily Mass, the major moments of people's lives, involvement of people as volunteers in parish life, a total religious education program from the cradle to the grave, a challenging and accountable, financial program, and an active effort to reach out to the hurting here and abroad. Their validity in one parish caused me to use them, a decade later, as start-up priorities when I became pastor of another church.

These priorities—both personal and professional—help deal with the tension of too many demands and not enough time. They enable us to use our limited hours, energy, and finances in the most effective way possible. Priorities sound pleasant on paper, but often require uttering or making painful no decisions. That means responding with: "I cannot do this, accede to your request, because something else ranks higher on the priority list. It is impossible for me to do two things. I must attend to the other obligation and thus cannot attend to your concern."

My niece Susan has recently returned to work at the magazine. Leaving her new infant and resuming her editorial tasks was just such a hard priority choice.

Carrying out priorities—personal or professional—calls for courage.

◆ ◆ ◆

A Quote to Ponder: "If you want to make good use of your time, you've got to know what's most important and then give it all you've got. . . . Anyone who wants to become a problem-solver in business has to learn fairly early how to establish priorities. . . . Establishing priorities and using your time well aren't things you can pick up at the Harvard Business School. Formal learning can teach you a great deal, but many of the essential skills in life you have to develop on your own."[12]—Lee Iacocca

A Biblical Role Model: Susanna, a "very beautiful and God-fearing woman," was placed in a compromising situation by two elderly judges blinded by their lust for her. She groaned, "I am completely trapped. If I yield, it will be my death; if I refuse, I cannot escape your power. Yet it is better for me to fall into your power without guilt than to sin before the Lord." She made the choice, suffered false accusations, trusted wholeheartedly in the Lord, and was eventually vindicated with her innocence upheld by the prophet Daniel.—Daniel 13

4

COURAGE

Leaders have—and have need of—many qualities, including patience and imagination. But not the least of the qualities the leader is likely to require is simple courage. The young John F. Kennedy wrote a book called *Profiles in Courage*. He greatly admired the virtue of courage, whether it had been demonstrated in battle, on a baseball diamond, or in government. He identified some of those who proved they could be counted on, who stood up—who had courage.

To anyone suffering a heavy burden, the Italians offer a single word of support—*corragio!*—an invitation to reach deep within yourself for the inner strength, the courage, to deal with the problem.

In the very nature of things, all leaders will at some time or other find they have their own need for *corragio*.

Lee Thomas
Vice President, General Manager of the Philadelphia Phillies Professional Baseball Organization

On the August day I visited Philadelphia for an interview with the Phillies' Lee Thomas, its citizenry were unusually enthusiastic about their National League baseball team.

A shoe shine man at the 30th Street train/transportation center commented, "I am starting to get excited about them again."

The sports section of local papers carried more and longer stories about the team's current success.

Personnel of the sales department at the executive offices could not keep up with phone inquiries about that night's game and future contests.

Such excitement about baseball has been absent from the Philadelphia area for perhaps a half-dozen years. The Phillies have floundered badly on the field and the organization itself seemed to move without clear, strong direction.

But now they had won twelve straight games and were on the verge of breaking a record for consecutive victories. No matter that they currently stood at six games below .500, that they were twelve and one-half games behind the front-running Pirates, that they were only in fifth place or that they had just recently climbed out of the cellar. Players, manager, coaches, organization staff, and fans all were wearing smiles for the first time in too many years and feeling upbeat about their beloved ball team.

Lee Thomas was the person most responsible for this transformation of a losing team into a winning club. He also could take credit for turning a dispirited, lackluster organizational group into a positive, efficiently functioning management unit.

Baseball has been this man's main interest from his earliest childhood years when he would grab a ball, bat, and glove at sun-up and run out to play all day until sundown. But Thomas also had talents to accompany his liking for the game, and at age eighteen he signed a contract with the Yankees.

"I could have gone to a few colleges," Thomas told me during our interview across a conference table in the Phillies' executive offices at mammoth Veterans Stadium, "but I knew that baseball was what I wanted to do with my life and this gave me a chance."

It was not, however, a story of instant success, but rather a study of courage and determination in the midst of adversity. Minor league professional baseball especially at the beginning (Rookie or Class A league) level is difficult. Long bus rides, minimal salaries, meager food allowances, poor or no clubhouse facilities, dimly lit ballparks, and small, inexpensive rooms in local boardinghouses abruptly bring young men dreaming of major-league stardom into touch with harsh reality.

Lee thus spent seven and a half years working his way up through the "minors" before reaching the goal of every pro ball player, the "big" leagues.

"I thought of quitting a few times. It's tough to go home after the season and have people asking why you are hanging on, questioning the probability that you will ever make it to the top. But I enjoyed playing and loved the game, so I kept at it."

For a year and a half during that period he hardly played at all. Was it because of a lack of talent or some incapacitating injury? Thomas answered, "No. I would like to think that the manager didn't appreciate the ability I thought I had."

He obviously did possess the necessary skills because Thomas reached the majors and stayed there for seven years, including one with the Angels during which he was named to the All-Star team. A knee injury impaired the concluding period of his active playing career. Thomas ended his days as a player with the Nankai Hawks in Japan.

In a sense, Thomas at that point started all over again in baseball with the St. Louis Cardinals organization. Thomas began in their system as a coach and manager, then moved on and up as salesperson, traveling secretary, and, finally, director of player development. His success in these fields expanded his vision and he imagined himself one day as a general manager of some major league club.

Adversity, or at least a disappointment calling for courage and determination, once again entered his life. The Cardinal's general manager post became available. Thomas certainly seemed a prospect for that job, since he had been appointed and was the acting interim general manager.

"But they never called, never asked me. I was there. I was visible, present. Our development program had been very successful and was well regarded by baseball people around the league. Apparently the powers that be didn't think I was the man for the job. The Cardinals had been good to me, but didn't even give me the courtesy of a phone call. That was a real disappointment."

Lee Thomas is a big, brawny man, tough-minded, and probably somewhat thick-skinned. But it seemed evident to me during our visit that this failure of the Cardinals to make any contact with him about the job opening has been one of the deeper hurts in his life.

The Chicago White Sox and Houston Astros later approached and interviewed Thomas for their general manager's positions. One of those clubs nearly selected him for the post.

Finally, the Phillies contacted Thomas and named him as vice president, player personnel, then vice president-general manager in the summer of 1988.

"I knew the situation was bad here, but upon arrival I discovered that things were worse than I had anticipated. However, coming in July gave me an excellent opportunity to learn about the situation firsthand. I visited every farm team, sat through games, and spent time in the clubhouse. I decided to make no changes until I understood the entire operation." Once Thomas had a clear picture of the scene, he began his moves, including the dismissal of some personnel.

"I don't think anyone likes to fire others, but that is part of the job. In one case, I spent a long time deciding about the right person for a particular job and hired that individual. Unfortunately, it didn't work out and I had to let him go."

Lee Thomas predicted that it would take three years to turn matters around. He was right. During the first two years the Phillies were under .500 on the field, although some progress could be detected.

"That was tough," Thomas admits. "I hate to lose. It was hard going home each night having your brains beaten out. But we kept working at it."

Truly loyal fans could discern some improvement in the Phillies, but the 1991 season, supposedly when the turnaround would occur, began disastrously. Thomas found it necessary to fire the manager he had hired; the team played horribly; USA TODAY predicted the general manager's dismissal; the team's star player severely injured himself and another teammate in an alcohol-related automobile accident; and a second front-line player "was a big disappointment" in performance. The team wallowed in last place, and the local media, particularly one radio station, were unmercifully critical of the Phillies organization.

The fifty-six-year-old Thomas knew adversity again. But then came August and the winning streak (it ended at thirteen).

"We are not as good a team as a twelve-game winning streak, but we were not as bad as people said when we were playing poorly and losing seven in a row. This shows we may have turned the corner. If so, it is because the manager, the coaches, the scouts, all in the organization have done their job. Our plan is not only for the next year or so, but to develop a system that will produce good ball players for the next ten years."

Thomas considers himself in baseball to be a man of his word, truthful, a person of integrity. He hopes that those same qualities are transmitted to his two boys.

"Parents are the real leaders of the world." They teach by example, he says, and that would, for his children, include their father's example of facing adversity with courage and determination.[1]

Postscript: How did the rest of the season fare for the Phillies and for Thomas?

Some successes, some floundering, more adversity, more need for courage and persistence, and a bright light at the end of the dark tunnel.

For a short period their winning ways continued and the Phillies held the best record in the National League after the midsummer All Star break. Alas, then their star center fielder crashed into a fence making a spectacular catch, but in the process again cracked his collarbone. He was through for the season and another regular also finished the year

early because of an injury. Their departure and other troubles caused the Phillies' play to be inconsistent, yet they finished in a virtual tie for third place.

The light at the end of the tunnel surfaced in the Phillies'
farm system, the best barometer of any major league team's
future. In 1990, the Phillies' six farm clubs' combined season's records were the second worst in baseball. In 1991,
the same teams recorded a winning total for the first time
since 1980. They also made the biggest jump upward in
organized baseball, leaping from twenty-fifth in 1990 to
eleventh in 1991. Director of player development Del Unser
said, "We're getting to the point we wanted to get to. For a
while we were promoting guys hitting .210 and high ERAs
because we didn't have anything else."[2]

Three years of hard work, courage in the face of obstacles
and dogged persistence apparently is bearing fruit for the
Phillies organization.

"I don't think a manager has to win every division,"
Thomas remarks, "but it's nice to have the players in a winning surrounding. What were we last year with our farm
clubs? A hundred games under .500? So you have to be
happy with the improvement."

"Winning doesn't necessarily mean you're developing
players. But it leaves a good taste in the kids' mouths. If
there's anything we've done, it's change the attitude and I
think that's important. When you win, it tends to bring out
the best in players."

Consistent with his comments to me about the entire organization being responsible for any improvement, the Phillies general manager publicly credited Unser, field
coordinator Don Blasingame, and scouting director Jay
Hankins with the turnaround.[3]

The Pain in Change

Lee Thomas has frequently needed courage to cope with personal and professional adversities, courage to direct structural
and personnel changes in the Phillies organization, and courage

to make tough decisions. But those various tasks and that quality of courage are part and parcel of any leader's life.

Leaders by definition are agents of change, who seek to bring people from where they are to where they have not been. This means that every leader—from parent to pope—will need at times to possess great courage. Why? Because most of us do not enjoy moving from where we are to where we have not been.

Babies generally do not transfer willingly from the breast to the bottle. Usually little children cling to their security blankets, reluctantly stop thumb-sucking, and cry almost hysterically when dad or mom leaves them for the first time at nursery school or kindergarten.

College-bound high school graduates tend to feel both very excited and yet quite anxious during the summer months after graduation. They await the fall with its first few days of college and wonder what that will mean for them in terms of living in a new place, meeting many new people, and facing totally new responsibilities.

A change of job, house, or location is normally not accomplished without some tears and fears. Many people do not like to swim in water over their heads, walk in strange cities, or mix with total strangers. There is, at least in the beginning, some uneasiness with these new experiences.

Most people tend to develop habits of acting and patterns of thinking with which they are comfortable or satisfied. The prospect of altering the customary ways that they think or act will very possibly generate negative inner feelings.

An experience that is innovative and different can create excitement and offer relief from boredom. However, the same innovations and different approaches can likewise often cause people to feel reluctant about, and resentful of, the changes.

Once a change has been made and becomes an accepted part of our lives, we frequently forget our initial resistance to the change and our annoyance with the leader who pushed for the change.

Some Examples

There are many illustrations of this phenomenon of change in church life:

• People in the pews ordinarily consider that their Sunday financial gift is appropriate or even generous. The fact is, however, that few people give anywhere near 10 percent of their income for charity. Proponents of sacrificial giving who suggest that parishioners use the biblical norm of tithing (or 10 percent) as a guide for their donations (5 percent for the weekly donation, 5 percent for their other charities) will hit sensitive nerves and can expect some hostile reactions.

• Pastors who transfer from one church to another usually experience, sometimes without being aware of it, a deep personal loss and feelings of denial, anger, and sadness. Parishioners have similar reactions when they lose a familiar shepherd and must adjust to a successor, however gifted or sensitive the new pastor may be.

• Introducing parents to a different method of preparing children for First Penance and Communion, a system that involves the parents more actively in the process, will bring forth at least a few vocal objections and even open opposition, or cause fears and resentment that go unexpressed.

• Any plan to renovate an established church's interior purely for the sake of better liturgical worship and not simply for the purpose of needed repairs may well trigger highly emotional resistance from some parishioners.

• Challenging attitudes and actions, commonly accepted in our culture, but contrary to gospel and church teaching, will surely stir defensive responses among many.

These are specific instances of situations of change in the life of a Catholic parish—conditions that will call forth courage from those leaders seeking to bring them about. But, as we have said before, the essential Christian message does center around change.

Jesus' initial public proclamation as recorded in the Bible was: "Reform your lives and believe in the gospel" (Mark 1:15). The Lord commanded followers to be converted, to change their way of living, to turn around their manner of thinking and acting.

Moreover, the church, a human as well as a divine institution, sees itself always in need of change and about the process of reform. The Vatican II bishops explicitly noted that fact in connection with the liturgy. "The liturgy," they wrote, "is made up of unchangeable elements divinely instituted, and of elements subject to change. These latter not only may be changed but ought to be changed with the passage of time. . . ."[4]

Too Soon, Too Fast, Too Far

When I began writing and speaking about changes in the Catholic church during the late 1950s and early 1960s, most of us understood very little about how people react to an enforced shift in the way that they customarily think, act, or pray. There was almost no literature on the subject and few, if any, serious studies on human behavioral response to cultural or religious change.

But we quickly discovered that many persons suffered acute agitation or anxiety when the church, for example, changed its rules and ways of worship. Parishioners experienced rather abruptly and within a relatively short period of time radical revisions in the liturgy or their public prayer. The priest faced toward them instead of away from them during Mass; a vernacular language replaced the ancient Latin; the congregation was expected to sing rather than to remain silent. Those shifts and the inner turmoil caused by them often evolved into suppressed resentment or open anger toward leaders who were trying to implement the church's directives.

Eventually two best-selling publications appeared that provided insights into this process of change.

One was *Future Shock* by Alvin Toffler. This book, published in 1970, addressed issues and coined phrases like *the death of permanence, transience, novelty, diversity, the limits of adaptability, strategies for survival,* and *a social futurism.*

Toffler observed that it is not so much the content of change which upsets people, but the rate of change. Human beings, in his view, can respond only at a limited pace to shifts in their environment; when the speed of change exceeds their ability to adjust or adapt, severe dislocation and disorientation result.

This principle, Toffler maintains, applies to "different conceptions of time, space, work, love, religion, sex, and everything else."[5]

Toffler details what experimental psychologists term an "orientation response." According to that concept, when new ideas, sights, or sounds confront us, we experience a psychosomatic reaction. Muscle tone rises, brain wave patterns shift, fingers and toes grow cold, palms sweat, blood rushes to the head, and breathing and heart rates alter.[6]

Until this novel fact or way of doing things can be reconciled or our world view altered, Toffler argues that we will suffer such an unpleasant, unsettling orientation response.

A leader who is the change agent in this process will naturally bear the brunt of the people's negative reaction to the proposed new way of thinking, acting, or praying.

Experiencing Deep Personal Loss

The other helpful publication was *On Death and Dying* by Dr. Elisabeth Kübler-Ross.[7]

Dr. Kübler-Ross, a psychiatrist who directs the Family Service and Mental Health Center of South Cook County in Chicago, Illinois, wrote this book in 1969. It represents the fruit of her extensive research with terminally ill patients and details the five stages that deathly sick persons generally pass through in their last weeks, days, and hours.

Those stages, or categories of feelings, are denial, anger, bargaining, sadness, and acceptance.

Kübler-Ross also notes that these different feelings, moods, attitudes, or reactions often, in fact usually, occur also among members of the sick person's family and those close to the critically ill patient. Subsequent observations and reflections have revealed that these stages of dying or death apply also to people experiencing any deep personal loss.

Divorce is a primary example. In fact, many deem divorce to be more devastating than death because it entails hurtful personal rejection and frequently causes agonizing self-doubts. During the traumatic time before, during, and after the disruption of the marriage, spouses often suffer through moments of denial, anger, bargaining, and sadness before eventually reaching a certain level of resigned acceptance.

The death and dying stages apply equally to other losses such as dismissal from one's job, departure from one home to another brought on by a spouses's occupational transfer, and the renovation of a church's interior.

Willy Malarcher, a liturgical artist from New Jersey, never understood why he invariably encountered hostile reactions from a parish committee after proposing to its members possible changes in their church's interior.

After all, Malarcher thought, he had merely displayed pictures of renovated structures and cited official church documents in support of his notions. Only after a study of Kübler-Ross's ideas did he realize that the parishioners considered this proposed renovation as a deep, personal loss. They felt threatened with the death or at least wounding of dear old friends—like the tabernacle, altar, communion railing, and baptismal font. Consequently, they felt angry at him, annoyed at the pastor for inviting Malarcher, and sad at the prospects of change.

Again, leaders as change agents must expect this type of reaction and possess the courage to bear with it.

All progress involves change, but not all change involves progress. The bishops at Vatican II endorsed this principle, as it were, when they agreed that "there must be no innovations unless the good of the Church genuinely and certainly requires them, and care must be taken that any new forms adopted should in some way grow organically from forms already existing."[8]

Good leaders tread that fine line. They discern what changes will bring about true progress and know it will require courage to lead people from where they are to a new place where they have not been.

Making Tough Decisions

Lee Thomas had to make tough organizational and personnel decisions with the Phillies, changing systems that were not working properly and firing people who were not performing effectively. It takes courage to make such tough decisions. But Thomas is not an exception. Every leader will be called upon at least now and then to make tough decisions as in the following situations.

Tough decisions require courage when they cannot be explained because of confidentiality.
The leader may be in possession of facts about a person or situation which, for very good reasons affecting an individual or the community, cannot be made public.

A seminary rector, for example, after consultation with faculty advisers, dismissed a student because this particular candidate for the priesthood had some serious personal problems that would critically impede his ability later on to serve satisfactorily as a priest.

The dismissed student, angered by this action, made false accusations against the rector and claimed that an injustice had been done. Classmates and friends lent him sympathy and joined in decrying the seminary head. The rector remained silent. To reveal the actual reasons behind the dismissal would have ruined the departed student's reputation.

Six years later the former seminarian's addictive weakness led him into serious trouble, publicly known, a development that underscored the wisdom of the dismissal decision. Probably few, if any, of the rector's attackers returned and apologized for their unjust accusations.

The rector simply had to endure with courage that sort of criticism.

This has become a more intense challenge today. The media and the public they serve so demand open disclosure of everything that any claims about confidentiality are seen as ploys to cover up something which should be exposed to the eyes and ears of all who become judge and jury of everyone.

Tough decisions require courage when they are not popular.
Thirteen-year-old Joshua Elliott was an only child, a gifted student, a talented musician, and a young man living in the college town of Hamilton, New York, who already dreamed of going to Harvard. On a clear, warm April day he spent some time shopping and having a hot dog in town with his mother. He then left her to ride his bicycle home.

Debra Spurling, age thirty-six, driving under the influence of a .34 percent blood alcohol content, struck the boy down and snuffed out his gifts, his dreams, his life.

The anguish and subsequent anger of his mother and relatives was understandably intense and bitter. Moreover, both public figures and private individuals, crusading against the evils of drunken driving, quickly called for justice and incarceration of the "killer."

It was for county Judge William F. O'Brien to preside over the case and to see that the accused was given a fair trial in the midst of enormous publicity and pressure.

The jury found Spurling guilty of manslaughter and other offenses, decisions that meant a state-mandated five to fifteen years in prison.

Judge O'Brien then departed from his usual pattern of confining convicted felons to jail until sentencing. He released the woman on bail until several weeks later when she would be sentenced.

His action caused an uproar.

The local paper carried a headline: "Mother Shocked at Killer's Release."[9]

A subheadline read: "Woman convicted of manslaughter in teen's death is out on bail until sentencing."

The boy's mother experienced shock, "I'm devastated and I do not understand the judge's decision. To me, this is not a just decision. It's not just to the public, she's a risk to us. It's not just to her, if she's a risk to herself."

The district attorney, a Democrat, criticized O'Brien, a Republican up for election that year, for his decision. "I see nothing extraordinary to compel this court to take a highly unusual step in releasing her. . . . The risk to the public is too great."

Why did O'Brien take such an unpopular stand?

"We have to temper justice with mercy," O'Brien told me. "This was a tragedy, an untreated alcoholic causing the boy's death. But she is under supervision by the county's probation office, is a single parent, has an elderly mother who is seriously ill and a seventeen-year-old son. To have some time with them before she goes to jail, perhaps the last time ever in the case of her mother, seemed the right thing to do, the humane thing to do, with little or no risk to the public."

The defendant's lawyer said to O'Brien afterward, "Judge, that was a courageous decision you just made." He knew that the publicity would be quite negative and could hurt O'Brien's chances of being reelected in the fall.

Time will tell whether this tough decision in making an unpopular decision not only required courage but cost him his judgeship as well.

Tough decisions require courage when they are complex.
Leaders often must gather input from a wide variety of sources and hear quite different opinions from many persons, evaluate them all, and then make decisions they judge are best. That decision may be for a church, organization, institution, company, community, or country. The larger the unit, the more diverse will be the input and the more complex will be the decision-making process.

Our parish presently has 1500 families and a staff of 32, some of whom are full-time, most of whom are part-time employees.

The full-time staff members are dedicated, competent people who are anxious to fulfill their functions well. They have generated many, many programs to respond to the expressed needs of parishioners ranging from "Moms and Tots" each Friday morning to Funeral Guilds hosting occasional luncheons for bereaved families after the burial rites. But our buildings provide only limited space for meetings and other activities. Conflicts do arise. It is for the leader to facilitate with the staff ways of working amicably through those difficulties. Sometimes, however, the leader must make a decision when the conflict cannot otherwise be resolved, a decision based upon a wider or total vision of the situation.

A parish of this size, moreover, contains an enormous divergence of peoples and preferences, married and single, young and old, rich and poor, healthy and sickly, active and inactive. Parishioners also include people who would like to see the church change even faster, and people who regret that the church ever changed. Some would like to hold hands during the Our Father at Mass, whereas others strongly object to shaking hands at the exchange of peace. Some want to hear more about current events from the pulpit, and others think the church has already become too political. The list could go on.

It is for the parish leader and leaders to sort out all those needs and preferences and move in a direction that will serve the greatest number in the best way. Some will necessarily be displeased with certain decisions since they run contrary to their own wishes. Others will disagree with certain decisions and fail to understand them because their perspective is limited and they do not grasp all the factors involved.

In our times this delicate task is exacerbated for leaders of every type by common contemporary patterns of political pressuring. That is, interest groups organize and publicize their particular viewpoints, often with strident tones and media support. They in fact may represent a minority view, but their intensity and visibility convey the impression of a wide-based backing. It is for leaders to listen to such input, but also to solicit opposing views. Decisions made, unless they coincide with the thrust of the activist group, will seldom gain their approval.

Elected representatives bear a double burden. They must serve and speak for their own constituency, but also look to the needs of the wider community. For example, members of Congress who urge arms reduction or defense cuts and yet who represent areas with large defense industries must find this a particularly arduous and challenging task.

In a word, it is difficult, almost impossible to explain decisions made that have many factors behind them and which will not satisfy everyone. It takes courage to make these decisions and to stand confidently behind them.

Tough decisions require courage when though morally and theologically correct, they run contrary to the prevailing culture.

Parents must experience this frequently when they insist on certain rules for their adolescent children about driving, using drugs, or dating, and are told: "All the other kids are doing it. You are out of date, old-fashioned."

In one of our local towns the high school junior varsity basketball season ended when the team suspended nine of its eleven players for drinking at a beer blast following a victory.

Most of the players were fourteen to sixteen years old. Some of the boys passed out from drinking beer. Some had ten beers; others just a couple.

It seems odd to this old-fashioned writer that the host's mother was home during the beer blast. Did she approve? Did she foster it? One player said it was not the first time the team had gone to a party where alcohol was served.

A mother of one suspended cheerleader took a quite different stance, a courageous one I would think: "Well, if you break the rules, you pay the price. I'm glad they got caught."[10]

Preachers and teachers of God's word have known the necessity of such courage from the earliest centuries before Christ until our current age. The Jewish people of the Bible repeatedly grumbled at Moses' words, and John, the author of Revelation, knew persecution as did all the apostles. St. Peter gave his life as his Master did; Peter's successor centuries later, Pope John Paul II, nearly died from an assassin's bullet.

There is a leadership quality or characteristic connected to courage—the wisdom to evaluate criticism and respond appropriately. I call that quality in a leader scientific sensitivity and describe it in the next chapter.

A Quote to Ponder: "God, give us grace to accept with serenity the things that cannot be changed, courage to change the things which should be changed, and the wisdom to distinguish the one from the other."[11]—Reinhold Niebuhr

A Biblical Role Model: Queen Esther, instructed by her foster father to plead to the king on behalf of the Jewish people, even at the risk of her own life, prayed: "Be mindful of us, O Lord. Manifest yourself in the time of our distress and give me courage, King of gods and Ruler of every power." She then went courageously and at great peril to the courtyard of the king. However, he welcomed her. She thus was eventually able to save all of the condemned Jews.—Book of Esther

5

ON BEING A TARGET

As pastor of a church or CEO of a corporation, as school principal or parent, the leader is out there on the firing line. Leaders are visible, accessible—and natural targets for negative comments whether they are justified or not. For the leader, the challenge (often very difficult indeed) is knowing how to receive negative and possibly even nasty and hurtful comments and, even more importantly, how to evaluate them. How *do* you as a leader distinguish between valid criticisms that demand a response and, possibly, action, and unreasonable comments which you must simply endure?

Roger Cardinal Mahony
Cardinal Archbishop of Los Angeles

At a very early grammar school age, Roger Mahony learned to be responsible. He also absorbed his parents' faith and decided that God was calling him to the priesthood.

His father operated a poultry-processing plant outside of Los Angeles and his mother often labored there during the day with her husband. With such working parents, Roger, his twin brother, and older brother were expected to show self-reliance by sharing the household tasks of washing and ironing clothes as well as preparing meals.

The Mahonys were practicing Catholics, but not exceptionally devout ones. However, when young Roger took his scheduled turn to serve the 6:30 A.M. Mass at their parish, it was always his father who drove him to the church and stayed for the Eucharist. This visible expression of faith influenced the young Roger profoundly.

His family belonged to a large and flourishing parish. During Roger's childhood there were usually several young, vibrant, and outstanding priests on its staff. After divine grace, he says, he owes his priestly vocation to their example and encouragement.

Mahony entered the local high school seminary as a day student intending to serve later as a priest in the archdiocese of Los Angeles. But several things changed that plan. He had learned Spanish as a child through association with the many Hispanics employed at his father's plant. He also loved the valley area around Fresno and spent a good bit of time there with his mother's relatives. Not surprisingly, he dreamed of working as a priest among the Hispanics in general and with migrant workers in particular.

There was little likelihood that he could realize this goal of serving Hispanic migrant workers in the Los Angeles archdiocese. Consequently, he requested and was granted permission to be ordained for the diocese of Monterey-Fresno, where there was a better possibility of realizing his vision.

"After ordination in Fresno I was given a letter with my first assignment," Mahony recalls. "It read: 'You are assigned as assistant pastor at the Cathedral pro tem. On September 1, you will report to Catholic University in Washington for graduate work in social studies.' There was, of course, no consultation in those days. Going to school was the last thing I wanted to do. But I went for two years, received my Master's in Social Work and returned to the diocese as director of Catholic Charities.

"As it turned out, the degree was really valuable. I learned much about human growth and development as well as community organization—all most helpful information for the work ahead of me."

The then Father Mahony almost immediately plunged into the middle of a bitter and divisive conflict between the grape growers and the farm workers being organized under Cesar Chavez. He has vivid memories of that period:

"Those were terrible, terrible times with a tremendous amount of tension. Almost all the growers and workers were Catholic. Both wanted me, us, the clergy to take sides. Owners would threaten pastors, warning them that they would withhold their financial support unless they espoused the growers' position. The workers would feel betrayed unless we spoke on their behalf.

"We tried not to take sides, to work for reconciliation, to proclaim Catholic social teaching, to explain the rights of employers and the rights of workers. But it was very, very difficult. We had no idea how unknown the social teaching of the church was—or or how unaccepted it was."

Throughout the long struggle, Mahony was the regular target of harsh criticism. He even received dark warnings that he would be killed, if he didn't change his views or withdraw from the struggle.

"During that decade or so of conflict, including the grape and lettuce boycotts, I had telephoned death threats, my car had to be bomb-proofed, and the State Police took special care to protect me.

"In later years as a bishop I have, of course, encountered opposition or hostility, but these seem inconsequential when compared to the hate and bitterness of those days."

Mahony was still a relatively young priest when the pope appointed him auxiliary bishop of Fresno and, several years afterward, bishop of the Stockton diocese. At Stockton he issued two statements—one about disarmament and the other about the qualification of speakers or lecturers coming into the diocese—which drew some sharp criticism. Some of his associates claim that Bishop Mahony does not mind and even welcomes that kind of verbal opposition. What does he have to say about this?

"I think a leader of the church needs to give direction, clarity, and vision. To do so will, understandably, upset some people. However, the interesting and real background about the document concerning speakers and lecturers had to do with qualifications, not orthodoxy, and was intended primarily for Spanish, not English-speaking, presenters. At that time there were weekend Bible sessions for Hispanics and the people brought in to lecture were horrible. They had no qualifications at all and the content of their talks was simply awful. I tried to correct that with my policy statement."

When Pope John Paul II selected Bishop Mahony as the new archbishop of Los Angeles, he received almost daily, before he left Stockton, thick packets via Federal Express from individuals or groups in the city of Angels. These packages contained urgent demands that he take positions on a variety of issues, conditions, and policies.

"I decided that responding to these would be very unwise," Mahony told me. "Instead, I thought we needed some kind of comprehensive direction or vision. So once installed in Los Angeles, I convened a steering committee to conduct an Archdiocesan Convocation Process during 1985 and 1986. This group of qualified people developed a questionnaire to be handed out to parishioners on Sunday and completed by them at the end of Mass.

"We received over 400,000 filled-out forms. They enabled us to come up with a mission statement, a list of ten top pastoral priorities for the diocese, and a five-year plan to achieve them. Almost all of those goals and objectives have now been achieved, or at least steps are underway to accomplish them.

"Today when someone proposes a suggested action or program," Mahony said, "I can praise the recommendation and tell the petitioner that this may be an excellent item for the next five-year plan. At the present, however, it is not covered or included in our current thrust of activities."

How does Archbishop Mahony deal with nasty letters or critical comments?

"First of all, we have to put those criticisms in perspective. Secondly, I don't read or keep anonymous letters. If there is no return address on the letter or signature, I tear it up. I don't deal with it.

"We don't receive many letters criticizing archdiocesan policies or actions. Most are complaints about matters on the parish level. Since I have divided the archdiocese into pastoral regions and dioceses and appointed good people to be my presence in those areas, I send the letters to the local person in charge."

Mahony went on to say, "They immediately check to see if a copy of the negative note has been forwarded to the pastor under fire. If not, they write to the critic, inquiring if they have sent a copy or spoken with the pastor about the issue at hand. That usually takes care of the matter. We thus try to be direct and up front."

The archbishop received some negative press, locally and nationally, about accepting the gift of a helicopter and personally flying it around the archdiocese. The facts here?

"When I was in Fresno, a friend of mine had a helicopter that he used for crop dusting. I became interested and started taking lessons. But that stopped when I went to Stockton. After coming to Los Angeles I resumed instruction and obtained a license in 1988. The next year a group of laymen donated a used helicopter. I accepted the gift with an understanding that it wouldn't cost the archdiocese a cent to operate. We leased it to a company who added the craft to their fleet for rental when I did not use it. That income paid for its maintenance and operational costs.

"I enjoyed flying the helicopter and found it helpful around here. But after being named a cardinal (Mahony is the second youngest member of the College of Cardinals), some friends said that I shouldn't be flying any more; it is too dangerous. I thought about their comment and also reflected that my new duties make it harder to fly regularly. Unless you do fly at least once a week, it does become more risky."

How did he respond to his friends' criticism?

"I prayed over this and said, 'Lord send me some kind of a sign about what I should do.' Two days later, from out of nowhere (actually Napa Valley), a construction contractor sent us a premium cash offer for our helicopter. Signs can't be any clearer than that. So we have sold it and my helicopter days are over."

Cardinal Mahony has a few specific ideas about leaders:

"I think above all leaders need to surround themselves with good or great people who will not hesitate to speak the truth to them. Isolation is a serious danger for any leader. For example, my own cabinet of five persons plus the moderator of the curia are really the best people. This principle applies not only to the Church but to all of society.

"Leaders," Mahony continued, "also need to delegate— to let people around them move on their own whether they make mistakes or not. When I first came here, someone sent me a memo asking permission to buy 100 $.15 stamps. Leaders just can't be concerned about such matters. That type of micro-managing keeps leaders from their main tasks of creating a vision, stimulating ideas, and looking down the road five or ten years ahead. My people need to be self-confident, know what they are doing and avoid sending me memos asking for decisions they should make themselves.

"I also believe, particularly in the church, that we as leaders should give people the freedom to try things that don't work. For too long we have had a fail-safe approach, with a guarantee that everything must be successful. We need to try things, to allow experimentation and not to insist on only one approach to a situation or challenge."

Members of the archdiocesan staff shared at lunchtime time a story about the cardinal. Mahony, they said, was speaking to a group of affluent leaders at a prestigious Los Angeles club and urging them to share what they have with the poor. The response was reserved, even critical, here and there bordering on the hostile. Cardinal Mahony concluded by giving them his bedside phone number in case any of his listeners changed their minds and wanted to respond.

As he left the building followed by several of the audience, a person walking down the street recognized Mahony and spat in his face. The cardinal, who is now in his midfifties, never reached for his cheek to wipe off the spit; instead he turned, smiled gently, blessed his assailant, and said "God loves you and I love you."

That night, the story goes, his bedside phone rang and the caller, one of the skeptical luncheon guests who had witnessed the scene by the curb, said, "You made a believer of me out there on the street. How much do you want?"[1]

Thin- or Thick-Skinned

From his earliest months as a parish priest to his present days as chief shepherd of the mammoth Los Angeles archdiocese, Roger Mahony has been receiving and evaluating criticisms, and responding to them. But he or any leader must expect that type of treatment. Church pastor or corporate CEO, school principal or conscientious parent—they are out there, on the firing line, easily accessible and natural targets for people's negative comments.

In the earlier chapters on vision and courage I touched a bit on this topic. Leaders, trying to take people from where they are to where they are not, are bound to encounter opposition. Leaders who make tough decisions will likewise find that not all support their choices. Criticism goes with the territory. Any person giving true leadership will have critics.

Not many people I know particularly enjoy being criticized. But some find it harder than others to cope with critical remarks.

• We describe in the next chapter how individuals with especially shaky self-images may depend too much upon the approbation of others for a validation of their own personal worth. This tends to make them react defensively, and sometimes even too sensitively, to criticism.

• Those in the helping professions, such as pastors or teachers, whose work is intimately linked to their personal lives may find criticism about their performances more than usually hard to take because criticism of their work seems like criticism of them as private persons.

This, for example, has been a real challenge to the clergy, particularly celibate Roman Catholic clergy, over the years. The individual characteristics of every priest—his spirituality, maturity, personality—necessarily overflow into his ministerial functions. During the decades since the Second Vatican Council, some church leaders and theologians have, with good reasons,

tried to disconnect what they judged to be too close a link between the personhood and the priesthood of an ordained man.
But in fact that linkage between man and priest—or between the
man as a human being and the man as a functioning priest—
continues for many parishioners—and indeed for clergy as well.
The result is that criticism of a priest's homily or one of his
pastoral decisions, to cite two illustrations, can be taken by the
priest as criticism of him as a person.

• New and inexperienced leaders may react too swiftly to a
negative observation or specific complaint. They have not yet
learned this hard lesson of political life or acquired this wisdom
of the ancients: no one can please all the people they lead all the
time.

Iceberg or Ice Cube

But how does a leader best react to criticism?

Somewhere along the course of my thirty-six years in the
priesthood I discovered the notion of "scientific sensitivity" as a
good response to negative comments.

This approach demands that we listen carefully, with sensitive
respect, to the person making the critical remark. Then we at-
tempt to rephrase for the critic in our own words and gestures
the thoughts and feelings expressed to us. Finally, we thank her
or him for honesty and forthrightness. Those steps, however, are
easier to write down on paper than to carry out in practice.

Once those measures have been followed, the scientific side of
the response takes over. We have to evaluate both the criticism
itself and its source. Does the comment have validity? Is it one
person's negative opinion or does this individual represent a
significant body of people who think and feel similarly?

Another way to ask the question is this: Was the criticism the
tip of the iceberg or an isolated ice cube?

If it is the tip of the iceberg, than as a leader I have moved
too fast, too far, too soon, and I must pull back, analyze the
situation again, and consolidate whatever progress I have made.

If it is an isolated ice cube, then as a leader I should gently, but firmly, move forward, aware that never will everyone concur in any step we take.

The following story illustrates the point.

Group Home Controversy

Around 1980, New York State's Social Service Office sought to establish a "Group Home" for developmentally disabled persons in our community. At the time, this step was in the forefront of a national movement to deinstitutionalize people with such disabilities. The agency's executives hoped—and had good research to support those hopes—that this move to locate a small cluster of these persons in a residential home would be more humane, enhance the quality of their lives, and, surprisingly, be much less expensive than maintaining them in a large institutional center.

Some of the people in the community objected strongly, fearing a depreciation in their property values and a threat to the neighborhood's security. Fortunately, clearer heads prevailed and the state moved ahead with its plans.

The fears proved to be totally groundless. The residents of the home tended to be even quieter and more reserved than other neighbors, and competent supervisors were always on hand. Property values never dropped and the small number of residents simply became an accepted part of the community.

Four of the residents were Roman Catholics who immediately entered into the life of our parish. Each Sunday a supervisor transported them up the hill to the church for Mass. In addition, our human development committee made it a point to have them as guests at our Pot Luck Production social nights, and as helpers cutting out angels for the large Christmas-giving tree project.

A dozen years later these residents had aged and were finding it increasingly difficult to climb the stairs of their two-story group home residence. The state agency in charge, responding to this new challenge, initiated the process of purchasing a one-story ranch house in one of the more affluent neighborhoods of our community and parish. The same earlier fears resurrected and several dozen citizens, some intensely irate and vocal, signed a petition opposing the proposal.

With the help of our parish social service director, I prepared a supportive statement for her to read at the public hearing. During that session, those opposing the new and additional group home expressed their views in bitterly angry terms. It was a tumultuous evening.

To our surprise, the town board, clearly moved by the objections, voted six to one against the state's plan—telling the state to look elsewhere for the desired group home.

Our staff were disappointed and angered by the board's decision. But we judged that a simple, organized letter-writing campaign by concerned parishioners to the board members would cause them to reconsider. However, to the staff's dismay and my own we quickly detected people's reluctance to become involved. Our request for letters often received polite, "I want to think about this" reponses. It seemed that there was widespread indifference among some of our parishioners and hardened opposition from others.

We concluded that I needed to address from the pulpit the basic issue of welcoming strangers to our community and offering homes to the homeless. I would have preferred to resolve this matter quietly because I was reluctant to use the pulpit for such a specific, concrete, localized concern. The Christian message is clear and definite—we must follow those words of the Lord about housing the homeless. But purchasing a particular home for a particular purpose is merely one way of carrying out that mandate, and not the only, nor necessarily the best way of doing it. Still, there appeared to be no other alternative.

Before I spoke I met with the town supervisor, talked in person or on the phone with each town board member, examined all the documents, and visited with the state agency's representative. Then I put together a four-page question-and-answer flier for distribution to parishioners on the weekend of the homily/ sermon.

The pulpit remarks took the "high ground" approach, recalling the biblical mandate to care for strangers and the homeless. I then urged residents of the affected neighborhood to "fear not,"—for what they feared would be a blight on their lovely section of the community could be a blessing instead. My homily urged the board members both to vote with courage and to represent their constituents. I urged parishioners to take the flier home, read it over, and, if they agreed with my support of the state's proposal to call or write their board member by Tuesday noon of that week (the next scheduled meeting of the board was on Tuesday night).

What happened? Each board member received twenty to fifty phone calls. A raft of supportive letters arrived at the town supervisor's desk, one third of them coming from residents of the neighborhood in question. A dozen or so articulate parishioners attended the board meeting (the opponents were there as well) and spoke on behalf of the motion.

The board reversed its decision by a unanimous vote.

What are the lessons to be learned from this case?

• In this case those opposing the additional group home, understandably fearful and very outspoken on the issue, were nevertheless not the tip of the iceberg, but isolated ice cubes.

• Good people sometimes must be stirred from their complacency and spurred on to act in support of beliefs that they actually hold deep down within themselves.

• The silent majority, once aroused, can and do make a difference.

• Elected leaders have the especially difficult task of distinguishing between the tip of the iceberg and the isolated ice cubes. To their great credit, our town board realized that they had misread matters and shifted their vote accordingly.

• Religious leaders may need to speak out, even if it means the loss of a few or many followers. In this instance, I received considerable verbal and written support from parishioners. Moreover, there was almost no criticism expressed to me personally. Still, I heard second-hand grumblings about mixing politics and the pulpit. I also received an anonymous note in the mail from one annoyed parishioner and read one letter to the editor in the local paper from a parishioner criticizing my views.

• Despite the remarkable reversal and success of an effort like this, leaders may still tend to dwell later on those few negative comments rather than upon the massive positive support. I examine this phenomenon in the next chapter.

Objective Evaluation of Criticisms

Criticisms will come to leaders almost automatically and without solicitation. But how do leaders obtain objective feedback, honest evaluations, and constructive comments about words that they have spoken, decisions that they have made, and actions that they have taken? Effective leadership needs this kind of useful feedback. How can we secure it? Here are a few suggestions:

• The leader's attitude of basic openness to any feedback—positive or negative—is essential. People who judge that a leader is truly seeking honest opinions are much more likely to provide them.

• The way leaders phrase the request for comments may hinder or help the process.

"How did you like my (talk, decision, action . . .)?" indicates that the leader is seeking support and affirmation. That makes it very difficult for someone to respond honestly.

"What did you think or how did you feel about my (talk, decision, action . . .)?" is less a solicitation for praise. It's easier in this case for someone to reply honestly. But even here "body language" or wordless expressions by the leader can get in the way of an objective response. The leader's face or gestures may reveal a need for support or a vulnerability to criticism. Sensitive respondents may catch that communication and dilute their honest criticism.

• Leaders who set up systems or structures designed to facilitate forthright feedback will very likely get it.

—Some commanding officers in the armed forces make it a point at regular staff meetings to solicit frank comments about a situation under discussion or to be faced. Subordinates who do not speak up honestly are judged ultimately to be lacking in a quality necessary for advancement in their careers. But once an honest review of a situation has been made and a decision taken, *then* the leader in command expects all to follow.

—Anonymous written evaluations will also promote a more accurate expression of people's views.

After teaching a once-a-week class on marriage for an entire year to high school seniors two decades ago, I gave them during the last session a short form upon which to critique the course. No names were required or desired. The questions were:

"How do you rate the course? Terrific, good, so-so, or lousy?" (Circle one)

"What did you like most about the course?"

"What did you like least about the course?"

"Can you cite one particular idea or notion that you gained during the course?"

I drove home rather anxious and excited in anticipation of reading the presumably positive responses.

The first evaluation went this way:

Rating of the course: "Lousy"

Like most about the course: "The last class"

Like least about the course: "The first class"

One particular idea or notion learned: "How to cope with boring situations."

So much for affirming, anonymous feedback.

But when I totaled the responses, there were eight excellents, sixteen goods, one so-so and the one "lousy" response.

In this case, again, the one "so-so" and one "lousy" were not tips of the iceberg evaluations, but minority, isolated ice cubes.

How we react personally to the "so-so" and "lousy" replies, even though they represent isolated ice cubes, is also discussed in the next chapter.

A basically open attitude, with neutral questions and an easy system for responses, will provide good feedback on past decisions or actions—and quite possibly a helpful basis for future action.

Making Decisions

Making wise decisions and living well with those we have made are fundamental tasks or responsibilities for every leader.

Those decisions may center around major matters. The president must choose between signing or vetoing a controversial bill. A top corporation officer must decide whether to invest huge sums in a potentially profitable, but risky venture, or to move cautiously and preserve cash. Someone must decide whether or not to marry a particular partner; someone else must opt for or against radical surgery.

Other decisions may involve lesser, but still substantive items such as choosing a college, buying a house, or retiring.

Some decisions may be no more momentous than the selection of a restaurant, or a movie, or a plan for spending the day.

Usually we are not comfortable or at rest with ourselves until we have made those decisions. Yet, we need to resist the temptation to dispel that uneasiness by making too-swift and possibly bad choices. The leader's goal, of course, is to make wise judgments. Here are some guidelines for making those kind of decisions.

1. *Talk with everyone who will be affected by the decision, at least to the extent that you can.*
This process produces valuable input for reaching the decision. It also gives those you contacted a true feeling of participation in the decision that is eventually made.

The authors of *Megatrends* maintain that the United States has moved in the past decades from a representative to a participative democracy. According to this theory, in former times we elected our delegates and then simply accepted their decisions as the product of intelligent, wise, and concerned people. Today, instead, the electorate in effect warns representatives: "If a major decision under consideration is to affect us personally, then you must consult us about it."[2]

We have seen this trend surface in the church. Previously a bishop or pastor's decision about a school or parish, for example, might generate a few critical public comments, but generally the opposition would be limited to informal, private grumbling. Today, opponents do not hesitate to speak out or even organize formal campaigns against propositions that will affect them.

This phenomenon makes broadly based consultation prior to a leader's decision all the more critical. Likewise, the concept of decision making by consensus—held by many to be the ideal procedure in our contemporary church—presupposes just such prior discussions.

In some cases, those preliminary consultations may make the ultimate decision obvious; or, indeed, they may make clear that someone else, following the principles of subsidiarity, should make the decision rather than the leader. The leader's decision, in that latter case, is to decide that someone else should make the decision.

2. *Find out all the facts.*

The consultative process described previously does produce much information about the decision under discussion. Nevertheless, there may be other sources of data crucial to allow one to make a wise decision.

As an illustration, I would like to return to the "Group Home" controversy in our community discussed earlier in this chapter.

After deciding (with real reluctance but with peaceful certainty) that I would need to address the issue from the pulpit, I went on a three-day fact-finding mission, speaking with the involved persons and reading up on the subject. My search revealed:

That the town supervisor was in favor of and had cast the lone vote on behalf of the Group Home;

That one board member who voted negatively had been replaced through the elective process by a new member who felt positive about the home;

That another board member had already shifted her position;

That the state had granted a two-week extension, making a revote possible;

That the board members, in the initial balloting, had not realized that their negative vote would cost the town a considerable sum in legal fees to justify their decision;

That the house to be purchased was unoccupied and had been on the market for more than a year, meaning that no one was being ousted from their home;

That there were only 5 group homes in the community or one for every 1500 residents—hardly a saturation situation;

That cost to the taxpayers would be only $.06 per $1000 assessment;

That a thick book of case studies carefully documents that no decline in property values of nearby homes has occurred when a group has been established in a neighborhood;

That only thirty-one, not fifty names were on the objecting

petition, including two very elderly persons, the meaningfulness of whose signatures and opposition could be questioned;

That there were people in our parish quite willing to write strong letters of support.

In other words, we had a good case, with strong supporting arguments. We needed only one vote to reverse the stand. We could propose reasonable alternatives for the board members to follow as an "out" or to save face; and accordingly we had a solid possibility of reversing the vote.

One must take such social stands for justice, even if they are neither popular nor successful. But it obviously helps when there is a real possibility for success. Having the facts helped in this circumstance produce a positive result. Having the facts also helps a leader make wise decisions.

3. *Take time aside and find a quiet place to reflect upon the consultation and facts, to weigh the alternatives or impact, and to make the decision.*

Leaders obviously do not, cannot, and should not follow this third step with every decision, only with the major or more significant issues.

Peter Drucker's recommendation, cited in an earlier chapter, supports this approach. For an executive to stay home during a morning, or go off in the afternoon or hold all calls for an hour with the office door closed—these are ways to provide those moments for quiet contemplation.

Christian leaders add prayer for guidance into this decision-making procedure. They observe the first two steps—using all human efforts to help with the judgment, but then seek divine assistance in sorting out the issues at stake.

These people have many biblical examples or models to follow for their prayerful decision reaching. The first disciples of Christ, during the nine days between Ascension Thursday and Pentecost, were constantly at prayer, asking for guidance and courage during that difficult and troubling period of their lives.[3]

A brilliant friend and colleague of mine tends to make decisions more with his head than his heart. He is more likely to follow his reason than his feelings. He once said to me: "I am not interested in impressions. What I want is hard data." That quite bluntly describes scientific sensitivity—an openness to hear others' thoughts and catch their feelings, but a wisdom in evaluating this data. It regularly asks: Is this the tip of the iceberg or an isolated ice cube? Leaders who have developed the skill of scientific sensitivity are in better positions to make wise decisions.

A Quote to Ponder: "Test your premise. Test your media. Test your headlines and your illustrations. Test your level of expenditure. Test your commercials. Never stop testing and your advertising will never stop improving."—Thomas J. Peters and Robert H. Waterman, Jr.[4]

A Biblical Role Model: St. Paul frequently prayed for guidance and he preached about discernment, the ability to distinguish between different kinds of spirits—those from God and those from other less noble sources.—1 Corinthians 12

6

SELF-ESTEEM

A healthy self-image, neither overblown nor understated, is a great asset for a leader. Leaders who are sure who they are find it easier to delegate responsibility and to surround themselves with strong and talented associates. The confident leaders can also admit they were wrong, change their views, take risks, go against the flow, and endure criticism.

But a healthy self-esteem is more often a goal we seek than a happy state we achieve. Most of us, at some time or other, may encounter situations in which we have to work at reinforcing and sustaining a positive image of ourselves.

John D. Plumley
Successful Businessman, Elected Legislator, Chief County Executive

"Welcome to Camden, Queen Village of Oneida County." That sign greets visitors as they drive into this town of about 5000 nestled along the foothills of the Adirondack Mountains in upper New York State. Throughout his more than sixty years Jack Plumley has lived in Camden and always lived at the same 52 Elm Street address.

He recently retired as Chief Executive for Oneida County and has resumed full-time directorship of his several business ventures in the Camden area.

His extended service as county executive was merely the

culmination of Jack's long involvement in civic affairs. It started when he successfully ran for trustee of the Queen Village. It continued over the decades as he was elected and reelected a county legislator, chosen to be the body's majority leader, selected as chairman of the legislature, and appointed commissioner of Public Works. Finally, he was named, later to win election and reelection, as chief executive of Oneida County from 1983 to 1991.

Jack has also been a very successful businessman and entrepreneur—operating and eventually owning a landmark hardware store, developing the Mad River Realty Corporation, and starting the J. D. Plumley Construction Company. His is a real-life story of accomplishments that is as surprising as any Horatio Alger wrote.

Plumley's mother, Bessie, had come down to the village as a young girl from her family's Florence Hill farm just north of Camden in the early part of this century. She sought and found employment there as a domestic servant for one of the town's wealthier families. She also met and married Jack's dad, LeRoy, who had gone to barber school, but, not caring for that trade, went to work for the local power company.

They raised five children, the youngest of whom was this future public servant, born in 1929.

A tragic incident and severe hardship struck the family when Jack was a very young boy. Plumley describes the accident and the aftermath:

"My father worked as a lineman. In one of those accidents that happen, a pole broke, killing his companion and seriously injuring my dad.

"My parents were old school and would not accept any assistance. Remember that was at the height of the Depression. My mother took in washing and ironing to raise money so we could live and they could pay their bills. They did, too, every one of them, sometimes taking care of their debts with a weekly or monthly payment of only 50 cents.

"I can remember," Jack told me, "carrying those clothes on my hand sled in the winter and coaster wagon in the summer to and from homes of people in Camden. Florence

Stone, the long-time editor of our local paper, was one of mother's customers.

"Mother also would do housework for people and that contact eventually opened up a door for us. One of her employers served as president of the school board at a time when they were constructing a new building. There was some vandalism, and the powers that be decided that they should hire a night watchman. The president contacted my father and gave him the job despite the fact that dad's leg and arm were in casts.

"I was five then," Plumley recalls. "Each evening we would transport my father to the school and I would stay with him, be his mobility by running down those corridors checking rooms and doors. When the construction was completed and dad had recovered, he became the custodian or janitor and held that post from 1934 to 1950."

When Plumley reached thirteen, a person and a place entered into Jack's life that were profoundly to touch his future. The person was Joseph Alexander McFern, a Scotch-Irish Florence farmer and town supervisor who had recently sold his country land and bought a business in Camden. The place was McFern's (later Carpenter's) Hardware Store on Main Street. Plumley remembers well his beginnings there:

"One day I walked into the store and Joe handed me a broom, saying, 'Johnny if you want to work here, you have to start by sweeping the floor.' It was as simple as that. He was an elder statesman in the political arena and had also done quite well financially with his farm enterprises. As a result, many people came into the store to see Joe. I often watched the bargaining in our back room office as he loaned money to farmers, underwrote mortgages, helped out small lumbermen, and even bought raw furs in the spring. There were no written deals. His word was his bond; his handshake was it."

The store was not only a school for Plumley during which he learned about street-smart politics, negotiations, and fidelity to one's promises. It also provided an ideal location in which his natural characteristics surfaced, grew, and flourished: a winning smile and facile sense of humor; a friendly personality and interested ear; above all, an ability to make all who stopped to shop feel that Jack was deeply concerned about their lives.

After high school, Plumley went on to work full time at the hardware store before later completing a tour of duty in the service. After his return home, Jack resumed a position with the hardware store and attended college in the evenings. Soon, however, he had developed his own realty corporation and construction company. It was quite natural for Plumley eventually to attain first a part-time and then a full-time elected position in the county government.

This one-time sled and cart carrier of clothes and junior night watchman delivered countless speeches during three decades of service in the political and governmental field. In those talks, these words frequently passed through his lips: honesty, hard work, integrity, self-reliance, responsibility, truthfulness, and independence. It is not hard to discern where he absorbed respect and enthusiasm for those values.

But his parents taught him more than these bedrock virtues; they gave him excellent training in self-esteem.

"My dad and mom never completed high school," Jack observed as we chatted on a Labor Day in his office decorated with photos of the family and memorabilia of a long career in government service. "In fact, they probably had only the equivalent of six and one-half years of formal education. But they raised five kids and saw that we all graduated from high school. They instilled within us a great sense of pride. We had poverty of pocketbook, but no poverty of mind.

"We might have had less or done poorer than others, but our parents insisted that as long as we tried, as long as we had put forth our best, there was nothing to be ashamed of. We were just as good, just as important as anyone else."

After thirty-five years of public service, Plumley submitted his resignation as chief executive. He wanted to spend more time with his family, his three Camden businesses (he ultimately purchased the hardware store), and his favorite hobby—quiet time in the great outdoors hunting, fishing, and camping.

At a retirement dinner, the sheer number of people present, including dignitaries on both sides of the political spectrum, and the eloquent testimonies, said much about Plumley's popularity and effectiveness.

Speakers at the dinner maintained that every individual who ever interacted with Jack, from the maintenance person at a county building to the state senator of an opposing political persuasion, considered him a real friend. Such a remark would emerge naturally about a man who says of himself, "I have always seen a lot of good in everyone I have met."

Plumley, observers say, could be stubborn, a loner at times, and one not afraid to disagree with others. Jack responds to those comments: "The public deserves debate about issues. But my opponents are not good or bad persons depending upon whether they agree or disagree with me. Taking such disagreements personally is not healthy in the political field."

How did he cope with the stress of a top executive position? "Sometimes when I was having a problem in government and was starting to feel sorry for myself," Plumley notes, "I would call for my driver and go up to the Children's Hospital or the Association for Retarded Citizens or Broadacres. A few minutes at these places would take care of everything.

"I also like to go regularly to my camp in the woods. Years ago it was to hunt and fish. Now it is more to sit back and put things in perspective."

He and his wife Helen have seven children. Jack has strong feelings about the importance of parents giving good example, not displaying a double standard, and knowing that "your life has to be lived the way you profess to live."

Plumley's paternal words to his boys and girls, now all grown and doing well professionally in various fields, sound very much like admonitions he heard as a youngster from his own parents in the 1930s and 1940s.

"Take all the time in the world to make a commitment, but once you make it, keep it."
"If you start a job, finish it."
"Pay your bills."
"Honor your promises."
"Believe in duty, honor, and country."
"Cherish confidentiality, loyalty, dependability, and truthfulness."

Jack recently had one of those full circle life experiences. Wearing "his realty corporation hat," he took some potential buyers to view a home for sale in Camden. As he toured this large, older structure with the clients, Plumley pointed out a room and a back staircase down to the kitchen, then said, "That was where my mother lived when she came down from Florence Hill to work as a domestic servant for the original owners of this house."[1]

Jack Plumley's parents taught him many lessons about honesty, self-reliance, and hard work—to cite a few examples. But more importantly, they surrounded him with love and instilled within him a strong sense of self-esteem. As long as he did his best, they had said, he was as good as anyone else. In effect, they communicated that what you have done is not as important as who you are and how you have used the gifts given to you.

A positive self-concept leads to constructive behavior, for ourselves and for others. Jack's unique ability to recognize good in those countless people he has met flows out of his own ability to recognize goodness within himself. In addition, Plumley's comfort with himself as a person has enabled him to reach out continuously in service for others.

Conversely, a negative self-concept tends to destructive behavior, a life filled with actions that punish ourselves and others.

The Gentleman from Maryland

Plumley's childhood experiences helped develop within him a healthy self-esteem. Quite to the contrary, Robert Bauman, a former congressman from Maryland, had less positive growing-up experiences. They contributed heavily to the shaky self-concept within him that was later to cause havoc in his personal and professional life.

Those negative events began, in a sense, at or before his birth, for he was "the bastard child of an unwed mother" from a posh Philadelphia area.

The adoption petition papers described him as an infant child "destitute, unwanted, devoid of parental support and in need of care and protection."[2]

His adoptive mother was indulgent. She kept insisting that he was destined for some undefined greatness, and died when Bauman turned eight. His adoptive father was mild and also indulgent, but somewhat detached and an alcoholic.

This alcoholism led to a traumatic event in Robert Bauman's life, the occasion during which he first learned quite cruelly that he was an adopted child. It was a hot, sweltering afternoon and his father had pressed Robert into some household duties that the boy found particularly onerous. He ignored or bungled the tasks, igniting his father's temper. Bauman describes what happened next in his biography:

> Red-faced, sweating, and weaving from drink and the heat, he glared at me across the garage and shouted, "You know, if you don't straighten up and do what I tell you, you can just go back where you came from."
>
> Not fully comprehending this veiled threat I stared back at him with a quizzical expression on my face.
>
> "You know you're not my son, Bobby."
>
> I tried to catch my breath.
>
> His words were slurred but delivered with a clenched jaw that denoted contained anger.
>
> "Your mother and I adopted you when you were only days old."
>
> I felt as though I was smothering to death.
>
> He paused, as if to allow the impact to sink in.

"You better Goddamned straighten up because if you don't you can just get the hell out of here."

I felt tears rolling down my cheeks and quickly covered my face with my hands.

What he said so unexpectedly, important as it might seem, did not immediately hit me. Only later reflection brought on total sadness and expanded self-doubt. My first impression was confirmation; no wonder no one wanted me. My own parents, my own mother, father, whoever they were, had not wanted me either.[3]

Somewhat later Bauman read a book about the life of Abraham Lincoln. The story excited him and it gave him a plan for his own life. It suggested that he might have a future in law and politics.

Bauman recalls very specifically what transpired within himself after he completed the book.

Putting aside self-doubt, loneliness, low self-esteem, guilt about my sexuality, I now had a goal. I clearly recall making a conscious decision I was going to show a world that did not want me it would have to deal with me someday. I did not need anybody. If I was unloved, I would be respected. I would see to that.[4]

The drive behind this decision and determination indicated, as he notes, a connection with his youthful self-doubts and uncertain self-image. It also sent out warning signals about the possibility of destructive behavioral patterns in his future life.

Bauman did become a lawyer, did enter politics, did win a seat in Congress, and did gain fame as a brilliant parliamentarian. He also married, fathered four children, and became a Roman Catholic. He was seemingly successful in both his personal and professional lives.

But his conservative stance alienated him from the party in power and his caustic manner angered some congressional colleagues. Moreover, his addictions to alcohol and to certain clandestine sexual practices were being acted out ever more frequently, thereby becoming much more disruptive as well as dangerous.

In time, the Washington Metropolitan Police and the FBI investigated Bauman and confronted him with charges of illicit sexual actions. The matter became a public scandal and, ultimately, he lost his seat in Congress, his wife, his home, and his secure financial status.

Robert Bauman's lack of self-esteem from his earliest years, a product of forces largely beyond his control, seems to have been the major force behind those sad, tragic developments of his later life. In a personal letter to me some years after his book's appearance, he admitted that "indeed self-image is still a terrible burden and a roadblock to my future—but not the only baggage I carry."[5]

Sure or Shaky Self-Image

Over the past twenty years we have grown to understand how much our self-image impacts—for weal or for woe—our behavior. I have witnessed this repeatedly and frequently in my own pastoral ministry. The surface symptoms can be chemical addiction or sexual promiscuity, marital discord or adolescent rebellion, personal depression or emotional burnout. But some dialogue with the afflicted individual often reveals a poor self-concept as the root cause behind these external actions or attitudes.

Although for perhaps only a few, the struggle with self-esteem is a major battle and the exterior manifestations of a negative self-concept are serious concerns. Everyone at times must face this shadowy side of ourselves. Those encounters are more intense for some people than for others, and for any person at some moments they are more intense than at other occasions.

There does seem within all human beings this lurking tendency not to care about ourselves or at least not to care as fully as we should. That negative inclination then leads to discouraged, downcast feelings or even destructive, unhealthy behavior.

The questions that follow may help identify the presence of a self-esteem problem or at least to recognize the existence of some submerged dark shadows.

1. *How do you take compliments?*

People react to compliments in different ways. Some responses reflect positive self-images, whereas others reveal negative self-concepts. Some individuals wound the compliment givers and make them wince; others warm the givers' hearts and bring forth smiles. The following are a few of the reactions that wound or make the givers wince and suggest a lack of healthy self-esteem within the receivers.

• "The brutal brush off." Recipients in this response sort of stiff arm well-intentioned compliment givers, keep them at a distance, and act almost angry about the words of praise coming their way. The innocent compliment givers feel uncomfortable and awkward, wondering what they did wrong.

When we do not care deeply about ourselves, affirming words or gestures directed to us can trigger such defensive and hostile reactions. On a deeper, usually unconscious and irrational level, we somehow are ill at ease accepting the compliments. "If only you knew what I have actually done and the kind of person I truly am, you couldn't possibly offer such accolades." So speaks the hidden, dark voice deep down inside.

• "The humble downplay." Recipients merely shrug, perhaps drop their heads, and deprecate the deed done. "It was really nothing."

This can be a subtle request for a repeat of the compliment, or it might flow from a false understanding of humility. God casts down the proud and lifts up the humble, the Bible says. Should we not, therefore, a person replies, downplay our accomplishments?

A healthier spirituality argues that humility and truth are inseparable. Consequently, like Mary, the Mother of Jesus, we would do better glorifying God who has done such mighty things to and through us.

• "The quick deflection." Recipients in this scenario swiftly divert the compliment to another or others. "Oh, I have a great staff that make me look good."

This may very well be true, but the encomium was immediately and personally directed to the leader. The diversion could be more an awkwardness in accepting the compliment than a praiseworthy recognition of one's colleagues' contributions.

• "The faultfinder." Recipients take the compliment, but immediately cite a flaw in the object produced or the job done.

"The homily was O.K., but I messed up on several points in the middle."

That tendency to faultfind after a compliment is very common and a symptom of the need many of us have to work on building up healthy self-images.

2. *Do you tend to pick at yourself?*

Like the faultfinder, who whenever complimented, cites a flaw in the object produced or job done, are you inclined to dwell on negative comments rather than on positive responses?

Despite the fact that a criticism is clearly only an isolated ice cube and not the tip of the iceberg, do you find yourself continually reflecting upon that critical remark?

If a dozen people praise you with, "Nice talk, nice class, nice homily, nice dinner, nice job," but one person objects to what you did or said, is it your pattern to ponder that one objection and forget the twelve supportive comments?

My efforts with the Camillus Group Home brought forth almost totally positive verbal and nonverbal reactions. But my mail contained one anonymous, marked-up copy of the informational flier that we had distributed at Mass that weekend. My critic highlighted certain words in yellow—such as "pastor, meddling"—and printed along the margins a variety of comments:

"I have been a parishioner for over thirty years—and I'm leaving your church because of your own desires. Yours and my church has become show-time in Camillus. Cut-out the 'productions'—not needed."

"Why so involved for three people???"

"The pastor of St. Joes should stay out of politics. He has a captive group on Sundays to tell his own desires—preach the Word of God. *Not yours.*"

"Father, your getting too big for St. Joes. You should run for a local office—or get a real estate license."

Isn't it odd and symptomatic that, afterward, despite the success of our efforts and the overwhelming positive reactions, I seemed to carry these anonymous, negative remarks around in my head and felt troubled by them more than I pondered the supportive words and felt uplifted by them?

3. Have you a double standard with regard to vices and virtues?
To place a virtue after your name, must there be a perfect record with no slips and no failures? To place a vice after your name, is one blemish on the record, one slip, one failure sufficient?

For example, if you were asked, "Are you a patient parent?" how would you respond? If, upon reflection, you recall being quite patient with the children for six days, but remember erupting on one occasion during the seventh, would that compel you to say, "No, I am not really a patient parent; I blew it, I lost it on Saturday"?

4. Is there within you, at least unconsciously, a notion that you must earn people's love?
One of my nieces is a beautiful and bright, charming and energetic woman who has survived, always with a smile, many setbacks in her life. Some of the steps she has taken have not, by her own admission, been exactly in accord with Catholic principles and practices. (She married outside the church and was divorced, and was divorced again.) But I am not conscious of ever having criticized her actions or looked down upon her in any way. Uncles, after all, are meant only to love their nieces and nephews and provide them with presents.

At the wedding of one of her sisters, my niece and I had fine exchanges and connected well. Any distances between us seemed to have dissolved. Upon my return, I wrote to her and said that for me the high point of the wedding was this new closeness which appeared to emerge.

She wrote back:

> I want to thank you for your concern, support understanding and, most of all, *love* during our time together during the reception . . . It's hard to believe that it took twenty-nine years for us to get to know each other better. I guess I always felt—subconsciously—that I could only fall short of your expectations of me and disappoint you because the life I have led

(and am still leading, I guess) is not much in keeping with
the ideals I know you believe in. You showed me, at the wedding, that you have nothing but love and concern for me,
without passing judgment. I never gave you the chance before to let me know that, and it meant a great deal to me.

Did my niece feel that she had to earn my love? Did I communicate, in earlier years, a notion that correct Catholic behavior
was necessary for her to gain my total and accepting love?

5. *Are you able to let people love you?*
Just as compliments can make people with shaky self-images
uncomfortable, so expressions of love can make persons with
negative self-concepts uneasy. Again, the person subconsciously
mutters, "If you really knew me, my past, my present, my
thoughts, my desires, you wouldn't, you couldn't love me."

The film *An Officer and a Gentleman*, whose constantly coarse
language and too sexually explicit scenes marred the movie for
me, dramatized this reluctance in allowing people to love us.

The two lead characters both seemed driven to achieve because of poor self-esteem, of self-concepts damaged by totally
different parental experiences. The first had perfection-de-
manding parents who expected him to succeed and excel or else.
The second one had an alcoholic, carousing sailor father and
uncertain mother. Like Robert Bauman, the ill-fated congressman, this naval flier candidate drove himself relentlessly to win
his wings and prove his worth.

After the suicidal death of his friend, the first candidate, this
second one tried to cope with the meaning of these tragic events
and of life itself. As he paced back and forth along the shore of
Puget Sound wrestling with these issues, his girlfriend, seeking
to help, came to him and in a gentle, supportive way, expressed
her love.

He cringed, backed away, and shouted, "I don't want anyone
to love me!"

If we don't see ourselves as lovable, then such tender manifestations of love can trigger a host of nonaccepting responses.

Closely connected with this point is our attitude toward being
and doing. Hebrew culture, biblical texts, and Christian theology

stress that being is as important as doing. On the other hand, contemporary society tends to a contrary belief that one's existence is worthwhile solely in terms of achievement, production, and success.[6]

Consequently, both would-be naval fliers in the film appeared driven to excel in an effort to justify their existence and worth. They also responded clumsily in the face of love, one hungrily seeking it and being rejected as a person, the other being offered it and angrily rebuffing the giver.

6. Would you characterize yourself as deeply compassionate or excessively competitive?

One of the more popular Catholic writers on spiritual matters, Father Henri J. M. Nouwen, writing in collaboration with two other priests, maintains in *Compassion* that competition, not compassion is the main motivator in our lives. We are, they argue, "recognized, honored, rejected, or despised" by our differences and distinctions. Whether we are more or less intelligent, attractive, wealthy, and so on "depends upon those with whom we are compared or those with whom we compete." It is, they conclude, "upon those positive or negative distinctions that much of our self-esteem depends." As a consequence, these three men judge that "this all-pervasive competition. . . . stands in the way of our being compassionate."[7]

A metaphor may help. How do you view the world? Like a clear night sky sparkling with an infinite number of stars—each one representing a person whose gifts are being fully utilized? Or an enormous pie cut up into many, but still only a finite number of slices—each piece representing a person with her or his gifts and talents?

If it is the sky you see, then every star adds to the beauty of your vision. Thus, you feel glad when a star sparkles and you feel sad when one is concealed or fails to shine with all its fullness. When a person does well, achieves a goal, displays a gift, or utilizes a talent, then your world is better, the vision more beautiful, and you rejoice. On the other hand, when a person does poorly, misses the mark, suppresses a gift, or misuses a talent, then your world is less, the vision clouded, and you grieve.

If it is a pie you see, then every piece someone else possesses means less for you. Hence, you may feel sad at the gifts or accomplishments of others and actually feel glad at another's failure or lack of talent.

The sky view leads a person to be more secure, better able to delegate, swifter to praise or affirm, and less liable to speak uncharitably about others. The pie view, on the other hand, tends to make a person more insecure, fearful of delegation, slower to acknowledge others' gifts or accomplishments, and more inclined, because of envy or jealousy, to voice negative remarks about others.

7. *How do you handle hurts—passively, aggressively, or assertively?*
When someone wounds you inwardly by a hurtful word or deed, do you wince inside, but say nothing, withdraw, brood over the injury, perhaps speak about it with several other confidants, yet never confront or discuss the matter with the person who supposedly inflicted this pain upon you? That is a passive response.

Or in the face of a similar affront, do you immediately erupt and attack the other person verbally or physically with words or deeds that are personally hurtful to her or him? That is an aggressive response.

Or, when hurt by the words or actions of another, do you sit down with the other party and carefully confront this individual—succinctly and strongly communicating your distress, but still respectful of this other person? That is an assertive response.

Those first two reactions generally flow from a lack of self-esteem. In one response we allow others to violate our own inner space. Because we are not strong enough within, we fail to maintain a healthy protective wall around us and the hurt or wound penetrates deeper than we should permit. In the other response, our shaky self-concept causes us to respond angrily and irrationally, rather blindly battering the other without regard or respect for that other as a person.

The assertion reaction, contrariwise, flows from a healthy self-regard and, curiously, further enhances one's self-concept.

We generally must learn the assertion process and keep practicing to develop a skill with it. Even then, the procedure does not work as smoothly in practice as outlined in theory.

Still, these three reactions to perceived hurts can tell us something about our own self-image.

8. *Do you have an unusual need to be acknowledged or appreciated?*
It is perfectly natural or normal to seek and welcome acknowledgment or appreciation. The pertinent word used here is an "unusual" need, that is, an excessive or more than ordinary desire for recognition.

Thomas Merton wrote an award-winning, *New York Times* bestselling list book, *Seven Storey Mountain,* which described his conversion to the Catholic Church and life as a Trappist monk in the Kentucky Abbey of Gethsemani. This book and subsequent publications established him in the forefront of spiritual writers throughout the United States during the last half of the twentieth century.

But a contemporary monk, actually Merton's physician in Gethsemani and a man later to become the abbot of another Trappist monastery in New York State, saw within the famous author this unusual need for recognition.

He writes that Merton "was a man who had a deep need to know that he was appreciated and loved, stronger than average. . . . His mother died when he was six, and his father was an artist who would suddenly decide to go off to North Africa and leave his son behind. So he had to become emotionally free and probably more than he should have had to be as a young boy."[8]

When we are not deeply sure of ourselves, there can be an unusual, more than ordinary need to be reassured by others.

9. *Are there any addictive behavioral patterns in your life?*
When the inner self is restless, not content and insecure, then we may hunger for comforts from outside, often doing so, after Robert Bauman's pattern, in ways that are compulsive or destructive. Those attractions may be potentially disastrous, such as chemical and sexual addictiveness, or simply troublesome and annoying, such as irritating habits we can't seem to control.

The Twelve Step process, which was begun as a successful plan for dealing with the disease of alcoholism, has become a standard recovery program for almost every other type of addiction as well.

Patrick Carnes, writing about sexual addiction and the Twelve Step method applied to it, maintains that an addict has four core beliefs.

1. Self-image: I am basically a bad, unworthy person.
2. Relationships: No one would love me as I am.
3. Needs: My needs are never going to be met if I have to depend on others.
4. Sexuality: Sex is my most important need.[9]

Behind addictive behavioral patterns, therefore, can lurk this undercurrent that I am basically a bad, unworthy person.

After reflecting upon the previous nine questions, would you agree that we have a tendency within not to care deeply about ourselves, that we struggle with self-esteem, and that our self-concepts are often clouded with doubts?

Accepting Affirmation and Affection

If there is a tendency not to care about ourselves, there are, on the other hand, three strong reasons why we should—one philosophical, one theological, and one practical.

Philosophically, we can look for support to the Thomistic or scholastic explanation of the way our minds and wills, our cognitive and volitional faculties work. The mind, according to this system, is drawn toward the truth; when it discovers and embraces truth, a certain joy, satisfaction, and contentment result. The will is drawn toward the good; when it discovers and enhances goodness, a corresponding joy, satisfaction, and contentment similarly result.

Thus, when people praise, like, or love us, they can do so only because they recognize some good within us. For us to allow, welcome, and accept that affirmation or affection from others is to acknowledge and endorse goodness within ourselves.

For example, at a Marriage Encounter "deeper" or training weekend, one woman, spurred on by the level of trust engendered during those days, wrote a ninety-minute love letter to her husband. In it, she revealed many dark events of the past and ugly shadows within her which she had concealed from him. Although this was not the intended or appropriate purpose of that ninety-minute letter-writing exercise, her ability to self-disclose on such a level excited the wife. She could barely wait for his return from the place where he was writing her a similar lengthy note.

When he finally reappeared and handed his letter over to her for reading, she was deeply touched. "I was so overwhelmed by his love," she recalls, "that I realized that the good he sees in me, I must begin to see in myself, instead of concentrating on my dark shadows and negative sides as I seem constantly to do."

Theologically, we connect the love that others give to us with the love God has for us. The human love we receive is but a mirror of the divine love constantly shining upon us. That latter love is far more perfect, penetrating, and permanent than the former love.

Our heads tell us that "God loves us." However, our hearts better come to understand and accept this unconditional divine love through the human loves extended to us.

Human love reflects and imitates the much deeper and greater divine love. When we freely and willingly take in these various human expressions of love, we better grasp the breadth and depth of divine love that surrounds us.

Practically, we learn from the affirmation and affection received from others how to deal better with our own limitations and weaknesses. Friends or lovers do not care for us because we are perfect; they care for us just as we are, "warts and all." Similarly, God does not love us in spite of our sins and shortcomings, but because of them.

Parents, for example, tend to reach out more swiftly and respond more tenderly to their children when their offspring are in trouble. The Bible tells us that God responds similarly, noting how it was precisely while we were still sinners that Christ died out of love for us (Romans 5:8).

We do need to care for ourselves. Allowing others to love us, welcoming their affirmation and affection, helps deepen the appreciation we have for the goodness within ourselves.

Building Up Self-Esteem

A key notion in all efforts to strengthen our self-image is the recognition that we are unique persons. We accept the fact of being fashioned in a particular, individualized way by a God who looks at everything and finds it "very good." That includes human beings formed in the divine image (Genesis 1:31;27).

The suggestions that follow are simply practical steps which can sharpen our awareness of this God-given special goodness.

Examine your fingertips. No one else has that set of fingertips. There never has been, is not now, nor will there ever be a person precisely like you.

Consider your hands. They, too, bear a singular quality with those many lines running across your palms in various directions. How many people have been helped or comforted by these hands through a letter written, a hand clasped, a shoulder patted, a body embraced, a forehead caressed, a wound bandaged, a hurt rubbed—always in a style uniquely your own?

Reflect on your calling. When you look back over the course of your life and the way your career or your vocation has unfolded, would you not readily admit that who you are today reflects the influence and bears the imprint of countless people, events, and forces. No other person has traveled the same path or followed an identical scenario.

Ponder your heart. Are you, for example, very outgoing and easily affectionate or quite retiring and rather reticent about displays of affection? The human heart has such diversity and depth that only God can penetrate the core of our being and know who we really are. Yet there are always persons attracted to us, drawn by glimpses of those distinctive inner qualities that now and then surface through our exterior selves.

Look at the birds and the flowers. Jesus told his followers to observe how God feeds the birds in the air and covers the fields on the earth. Yet, he says, "How much more important are you than birds ... If God clothes the grass in the field ... will he not much more provide for you, O you of little faith?" (Luke 12:22–34; Matthew 6:25–34).

Check the hair on your head (or lack of it). While encouraging his adherents to be courageous and not to fear during persecution,

Christ cites the example of two sparrows sold for an insignificant sum. "Yet not one of them falls to the ground without your Father's knowledge. Even all the hairs of your head are counted. So do not be afraid; you are worth more than many sparrows" (Matthew 10:26–33).

This is not one of my favorite biblical passages. I am very aware that all the hairs of my head are numbered.

Listen to the prophet Isaiah. The Lord speaks through the prophet Isaiah to us: "Fear not, for I have redeemed you; I have called you by name: you are mine . . . you are precious in my eyes and glorious . . . I love you . . . Fear not, for I am with you" (Isaiah 43:1,4–5).

When we may be experiencing a down time in our life and struggle with a shaky self-image, it can help to spend a few still minutes in a quiet space repeating over and over, "You are precious in my eyes and glorious and I love you."

Embrace a compliment. Take in the affirmation and accept it with thanks. Perhaps even turn the praise around with, "I really appreciate your positive words. I worked hard on that (dinner, speech, class, paper, outfit, lawn, or whatever). Your words make the effort all seem worthwhile and give me a lot of encouragement." Embracing the affirmation so totally and, even more, graciously returning the compliment to the giver builds both your own self-esteem and that of the person who originally praised you and your efforts.

Relish love offered. When a friend or fiancé, spouse or relative expresses love for you in any way, hold on to it, cherish it, let it sink within and ultimately reach your own heart. These people cannot love you and communicate that love to you unless they, at least subconsciously, perceive a lovable goodness inside you.

Jack Plumley's healthy self-esteem, fostered at an early age by caring parents, enabled him to reach out in an effective way with a friendly concern for others. It enhanced his ability as a leader. Robert Bauman's damaged self-esteem, the result in part of many negative childhood experiences, crippled his efforts to reach out effectively toward others. It diminished his ability as a leader. Most of us struggle to some degree with our self-images, but we can all work with success at improving them.

A *Quote to Ponder:* "The more I talked to men as well as women, the more it seemed that inner feelings of incompleteness, emptiness, self-doubt, and self-hatred were the same, no matter who experienced them, and even if they were expressed in culturally opposite ways. . . .

"People seemed to stop punishing others or themselves only when they gained some faith in their own unique, intrinsic worth. . . .

"I had felt drawn to the subject of self-esteem not only because other people needed it, but because I did. . . .

"I've learned . . . that self-esteem plays as much a part in the destiny of nations as it does in the lives of individuals; that self-hatred leads to the need either to dominate or to be dominated; citizens who refuse to obey anything but their own conscience can transform their countries; in short, that self-esteem is the basis of any real democracy."[10]—Gloria Steinem

A *Biblical Role Model:* Hannah pleaded with God for a son and was blessed with the birth of Samuel. She later presented the child in the temple and worshiped God by acknowledging that all her gifts, including the infant, were from above. "My heart exults in the Lord . . . I rejoice in my victory."—1 Samuel 1–2

7

LISTENING

One of the key components of leadership at any level is the ability to listen well and thoughtfully. Leaders hear out angry customers, annoyed colleagues, frustrated children, workers with gripes, people in pain. They listen very carefully to both objections and suggestions, ideas and complaints. They can't hope to follow through on all the recommendations or resolve every unhappiness. But when the leader is *seen* to have listened, to have paid attention to others' thoughts and feelings and tried to understand and seek a remedy if one is called for, the reaction is likely to be positive and tense situations defused. The listening helps.

Patricia Livingston
Single Parent, Educator, Lecturer, Author

"To start with, I don't think of myself as a leader," Patricia Livingston says.

Ms. Livingston has served for several years as associate director of the prestigious Center for Continuing Formation in Ministry (formerly the Clergy Institute) at Notre Dame University. She has delivered keynote addresses and received standing ovations at national and regional religious conventions throughout the United States. She has conducted many conferences on "Sexuality, Intimacy and Relationships" here and abroad, and earned an "outstanding" comment from the film producer for her part in a current, successful, and highly acclaimed video educational series. She has written a series of articles and a book on spirituality that have drawn rave reviews, and been honored by *U.S. Catholic* magazine as the "Person who has contributed significantly to the cause of women in the Church." Despite all these accomplishments and plaudits, this single parent of three grown children chooses to say she does not readily consider herself as a leader.

Her hesitation illustrates again the tendency among us to limit the title of leader to powerful figures who are much in the public eye. But, clearly Pat Livingston has touched the future of many people. Moreover, she surely is a leader in today's world and in our church.

Patricia Livingston and I have been friends and colleagues for over a dozen years. I have always considered "listening" to be one of her finest attributes. She listens superbly well and teaches that skill to others very effectively. But Pat disagrees, to an extent at least, that this is her primary leadership skill.

"I would not, on my own, come up with being a listener as my strength as a leader. I would say that if I am a leader, perhaps it is in the sense that I am an inspirer. I think I have the ability to hearten people. I try to help people feel close to themselves, to have a kind of tenderness for themselves.

"I have spent time thinking about how I may do this," she says. "We have had various presenters at our institute recently talk about preaching and over and over again it comes out that preaching needs to be concrete. You have to use images, metaphors, and stories. I think that is one of my strengths. I am an image maker, a storyteller. I try to use metaphors that go right to people's own experiences."

One of those powerful stories Pat Livingston often uses at lectures centers around her son Randy in a Little League baseball game and the lesson he learned from his mother that "life is not fair." The metaphor, Pat remarks, has taken on a life of its own. By word of mouth and via audiotapes it has reached audiences as far away as Alaska and South Africa, moving hearers to write to her with their admiration and appreciation.

How has she became so adept at storytelling, at expressing metaphors that break open people's hearts?

"I think the reason may be that I am a listener to life," Pat commented. "I have an enormous reverence for the experiences of other people."

A professor of sacred scripture at the center translated Pat's analysis into more general, theoretical terms. Good preachers, the professor maintained, must communicate their own faith to others with love and connect with the faith of the others to whom they are preaching. If it works, it becomes a deep exchange between people. You can tell when that happens, Pat observes, by the eye contact, the body language, by the nodding heads, by the feeling in the church.

"I really believe that," Pat said. "I think that may be my gift. When I speak, I experience their courage answering my courage, their laughter answering my humor, and their willingness to try to go on loving responding to my own struggling to love. I think that the secret for me, if I am a leader, is that I tap into people. And, I am so grateful when they respond, when it's clear to me that people know they gave to me as I gave to them. I think it is the mutuality which is my strength. It matters to me very much that what I say connects to their life. I am not indifferent. I am not impartially, cynically parceling out my scholarship. I am very vulnerable to them and they reward that vulnerability by responding with the chords from their own lives."

At the end of a concert on the Notre Dame campus, the star musician told the crowd that it had been a wonderful evening for him, that they had been a really glorious audience. Pat was there and knew from her experience as a speaker that those were not merely trite and expected farewell words from a seasoned entertainer. His music had unlocked central experiences of the audience's lives. They were grateful and responded; he, catching their responsiveness, played better and longer because of it.

"As a speaker I know how hard it is to have a lousy audience, a frozen audience, a group of people who simply don't want to be there. On the other hand, when my audience shows a willingness to allow my images to break open their lives, I am enormously grateful."

That kind of vulnerability to an audience is risky. Lecturers such as Livingston tend to carry home images of the one harshly hostile critic and to leave behind pictures of the ninety-nine enthusiastically positive participants. Pat hates that about herself, and once wondered if it was a weakness to try to overcome. A wise friend counseled otherwise.

"Your great gift," she told Pat, "is that you care. Nobody could doubt that. Because you care they open up to you." It is precisely her open caring for an audience that evokes such warm responses. This "capacity for mutuality," this quality of being a "listener to life," has come, as we might expect, mostly from her parents, but also from Pat's own life experiences.

Her father, a West Point and Harvard Law School graduate, made the military service his career and eventually rose in rank during the 1950s to become judge advocate general of the army or head of the Army Legal Corps, headquartered in the Pentagon.

"Dad has a whole eagerness about life," Pat commented. "He just introduces himself to everyone, from the checkout counter lady to the gardener. It didn't make any difference if he was in the Legal Corps, dean of the Law School, or head of the committees of the American Bar Association. He thinks people are wonderful and fascinating."

Her mother is a "really phenomenal listener" and very interested in others, although quite private as a person.

She and her husband once attended a formal White House dinner, with Pat's mother seated next to a well-known, very visible, and highly placed government official. Pat was sixteen at the time and recalls in detail her parents' retelling of the evening experience.

"Mom's dinner companion monologued all night, extolling his virtues and talking about himself. I am sure he didn't even know my mother's name and never asked one thing about her own life. At the end of the meal, he turned to my mother and said, 'Madame, you are the most fascinating dinner partner I have ever had.' He was in fact, totally fascinated by himself and she just listened!"

Pat Livingston's life has not been devoid of painful

wounds and dark shadows. Still, even those troubled situations have been occasions of growth for her.

Her marriage in 1962 seemed a perfect match. She was a senior at Trinity College in Washington and, he, although not a Catholic, was a West Point graduate and later, a lawyer. They brought three children into the world, two boys and a girl, children who often now occupy center stage in some of their mother's stories or metaphors.

They ultimately settled at Sebring, in midstate Florida, where her husband built up a law practice. But things didn't go well between them and they divorced in 1975. Pat then started work on a Master's Degree in Mental Health Counseling at the University of South Florida. It was an arduous task, one involving a 200-mile drive three days a week for almost two years.

Her courses naturally touched upon communication skills with an emphasis on listening, asserting oneself, problem solving, and managing conflict. Although the goal of the degree was to provide Pat with marketable skills as a teacher or counselor, she pursued these classes for another reason as well.

"I took these communication skills courses also," Pat admits, "so that I could be a better mother, a better parent. I feel that parenting is the hardest thing I have ever done. At times over the years I have felt totally inadequate for this role."

But the degree in counseling and communication skills opened the door to opportunities that she could never have envisioned. Her spiritual adviser at Trinity had maintained contact with Pat over the years and was now teaching in a seminary. He invited her to conduct with him there a creative specialized workshop for all of the students. Simultaneously she also was asked to teach a short course on communication skills in another section of the country as part of a program designed for priests.

Those led in turn to regular lectures at Notre Dame, the development of presentations on sexuality, especially for clergy and religious, keynote addresses, talks, and workshops at an increasing number of conventions and convoca-

‖ tions, some writing, and, in 1988, her current post in South ‖
‖ Bend as associate director of the Center at Notre Dame.[1] ‖

Wisdom from the Past

I first met this "listener to life" at Darlington Seminary in northern New Jersey at a training program for several dozen church leaders assembled there from across the United States. She was teaming with John Lawyer, a personnel consultant, to present an intensive ten-day course on communication skills. I was one of their students.

The general principles we learned and the practical skills we struggled to develop have been enormously helpful to me in many ways ever since. However, those efforts stirred within me memories of simple lessons about listening that I had learned two decades earlier. They also brought recollections of leaders I have known who were good listeners long before students were studying communications as an applied science on college campuses.

After ordination in 1956, the bishop assigned me to the Cathedral parish as fourth assistant to the venerable Monsignor James P. McPeak, long-time rector of this downtown church. McPeak was already seventy-eight years old when I moved in and was still there when I moved out in 1968. He finally left the cathedral a few years later for health reasons, and died in 1972 after serving as its rector for forty-nine years.

This tall, raspy voiced, gentle man practiced a style of commonsense leadership distilled into three verbs: "Organize, delegate, and supervise." The four of us under him often jokingly remarked that McPeak's version of this sage concept meant a maximum amount of delegation and a minimal amount of supervision. In other words, "Don't bother me about anything."

However, on those few occasions when we did interrupt the benign priest with some pastoral matter, he would listen very attentively, then invariably respond: "Well, what do you think you should do about this?"

Years later I frequently reflected upon those encounters and recognized that any contemporary communication skills expert would praise the old monsignor's wise ways of dealing with people and issues.

I was certainly ready, eager, and willing during those early months and years of my priesthood, but quite nervous, extremely idealistic, and totally inexperienced. Fortunately, the other assistant priests at the Cathedral, quite tolerant of the naive newcomer, were great role models and wise pastoral instructors.

Father George Arseneau, in particular, spent hours showing me how best to do certain procedures and sharing practical insights that he had garnered during his own sixteen years as a priest. I always felt indebted to him for that priceless hands-on course in pastoral theology.

At one of our minisessions together, Father Arseneau said, "What people are looking for more than anything else is an interested listener."

That was a remarkable insight then, although a commonplace truism today. In the late 1950s hardly anyone had even dreamed, much less heard of Clinical Pastoral Education courses, workshops in communications skills, or degrees in counseling. Now seminarians must complete a C.P.E. experience as a requisite for ordination to priesthood, corporations send executives to conferences on communications, and trained counselors are everywhere.

A central thread or common ingredient in these three activities—C.P.E., communications skill building, and counseling—is listening. Father George Arseneau was right—people are looking for interested listeners.

Learning How to Listen

There have always been those with natural gifts for listening. Our society has come to recognize, however, that every leader ideally should be a good listener. Moreover, we understand that formal training can enhance an individual's ability to listen well.[2] Here are a few lessons and skills taught in those formation sessions:

• Good listening means truly caring about what another person thinks and feels.

• Good listening requires that we pay attention to what the other person is saying to us, focusing upon the individual's verbal and nonverbal communication.

• Good listening prompts a listener to lead the other to talk more, to expand upon what has been said, and to clarify unclear points.

• Good listening does not judge, agree, or disagree, but instead, simply tries to catch accurately and sympathetically the other's thinking and feelings.

• Good listening, also termed active or reflective listening, attempts to mirror back in the listener's own words and gestures what the speaker has communicated.

• Good listening leaves the speaker with the satisfying sense of having been heard in a correct and understanding way.

The one listened to may be an unhappy child or a troubled student, an energetic staff member or a disgruntled stockholder, an excited bride-to-be or a joyful first-time father, an anxious client or a dying patient, an angry parishioner or a complimenting pastoral council member, an upset worker or a person grieving over the death of a spouse.

Regardless of the situation, good listening never fails to halve a sorrow and double a joy. It reduces tension and allows reason to reign. It encourages movers and shakers, while still calming the cautious and critical.

There is more to leadership than good listening. But experience shows that effective leaders listen well.

A Listening Archbishop

Archbishop Daniel Pilarczyk of Cincinnati has done an enormous amount of traveling during this past decade.

The elected president for the National Conference of Catholic Bishops, he must yearly attend many multiple day meetings in the United States connected with that body of leaders. In addition, Archbishop Pilarczyk flies a half-dozen times each year to Italy or other countries outside the United States, summoned there by the pope to serve as the representative of the Catholic church in America.

Moreover, Archbishop Pilarczyk's archdiocese covers a significant portion of Ohio, from the Kentucky border on the south to beyond Dayton in the north. Ordinary pastoral calls alone require frequent car trips to parishes, schools, and institutions spread throughout that area. However, at the beginning of his term as archbishop, he embarked upon an ambitious project of visiting every one of the 250 parishes within the Cincinnati archdiocese.

These were not cursory stops. He generally spent an entire day at each location listening to various individuals or groups and praying with them. Covering some sixty parishes yearly, it took him about four years to accomplish this task.

"When I was named archbishop in December of 1982," Archbishop Pilarczyk recalls, "the criticism was or could have been made that during my entire priesthood I had had no parish experience. I was either a seminary professor or rector or an auxiliary bishop throughout that time. So I decided to find out something more about parish life."

He sought advice about this "listening" project from administration officials and archdiocesan leaders. They counseled him to inform pastors in advance that this was not an inspection, that no report of things said would be sent back to the pastor or parish and that no financial offering was expected or desired. After Archbishop Pilarczyk had conducted a few of these visits, the word swiftly spread among the clergy that they had in fact no need to fear or be threatened by them.

"If the parish had a school, I began there, spending five minutes in each classroom," the archbishop explained. "I would ask what they are studying, talk about that subject a little and then inquire if they have a religion class. When questioned about what they had learned in their religious studies, the boys and girls almost always quickly responded: 'God loves us.' Invariably the children would want to recite for me the commandments or some prayer that they had memorized. Later, when critics would protest to me that pupils in Catholic schools no longer learn anything about religion, I found it effective to cite one of my recent experiences in the classrooms, citing both the children's clear answers and their careful memorization of basic formulas."

His presence did not always bring smiles and joy. At one parish

after the customary evening Mass, a mother informed the archbishop that her daughter came home from school that afternoon
in tears and all because of him. The little girl sobbed as she told
her mom:

"We waited all day for the archbishop and he didn't come into
our room until the very end. And then he didn't wear his robes
or big hat. He only wore a black suit, just like 'Father.' And he
was bald!"

The archbishop, following the school visit, met with the clergy,
parish staff, schoolteachers, and any religion education instructors who were available.

"I posed two questions: 'What things do you like that are going
on in the parish? What things would you like to see happen here
during the next five years?' The second question really gave them
an opportunity to talk about what they didn't like that was going
on in the parish."

He had dinner with the priests, celebrated Mass for the parish,
greeted people afterward, and then sat down with the parish
council for an hour, posing the same two questions.

"When I returned home I dictated about a page of notes for
our file on the parish. Later, when I was into using the computer,
I instead sat at the word processor and punched in the recollections myself. Those visits were tiring," the archbishop admitted
to me, "and it required four years to cover all the parishes, but
the process gave me a great picture of the archdiocese."

He likewise pursued a plan to visit individually for an hour
with every one of his clergy. There was no agenda for these
encounters. The clergy were invited merely to talk with their
archbishop about anything of concern for them. This listening
project or process likewise consumed a good bit of the archbishop's time and energy, but provided him with rich data for
the years ahead and established his style of open leadership.

His interviews with the clergy began after completion of the
parish visits. With 300 active and 100 retired diocesan priests,
these one-hour sessions took the archbishop two years to finish.

"Some days I would do five a day—really too many," Archbishop Pilarczyk said. "To help them along I posed these questions: 'How are you doing as a person?' That gave the man a
chance to say if he is happy or sad, troubled or content. 'What

is your ministry like?' This opened the door to talk about his work. 'If you had to do it over again, would you choose to be a priest?' Occasionally I jotted a few notes for myself, but sometimes after several interviews in a row I would get mixed up about who said what."

Archbishop Pilarczyk knows his clergy, likes them, and speaks proudly of them. He calls each priest by name. Those listening sessions helped make these things possible.

Gorbachev the Listener

Mikhail Gorbachev is hardly mentioned at all these days, but it was only a short time ago that the star of this visionary Russian general secretary burst upon the horizon. In 1987, *Time* magazine hailed him as the year's most remarkable figure.[3] His concepts of *glasnost* and *perestroika* had formed hope around the world for a new kind of Soviet Union. The country would, under his leadership, be more open, more concerned about the welfare of its citizens, and less preoccupied with the spread of its ideology and system abroad.

At least citizens everywhere hoped for that development.

One wonders now, if Gorbachev foresaw then the radical remaking of Russia soon to take place.

Time's cover story about Gorbachev, however, revealed him as a man known as a listener.

A leading Russian sociologist described an encounter with Gorbachev before he became general secretary.

"It is incredible what power and drive emanate from him. . . . His vitality is extraordinary and yet, although you feel this tension, he is a good listener and waits for you to finish."

Once in power as the top leader, Gorbachev's listening style continued. He would roam about Moscow, visiting supermarkets, chatting with factory workers, discussing computers with teachers, and listening to nurses talk about their pay scale at a local hospital. His "walk about" type of leadership soon became famous. The general populace sensed that their secretary was an open and accessible person.

Start-Up Listening Sessions

That kind of stance as a listener can prove especially valuable for an individual who has just been appointed to a new leadership post. The freshly designated leader possesses a once only opportunity to hold a series of "listening sessions" for constituents. These gatherings, involving ten–twenty people and lasting for about ninety minutes, provide a forum for people to express their suggestions and comments before those who are leading them.

Because the new leader is generally unknown and has made no major decisions, the "speakers" will feel freer to make their observations. One year later they will be more guarded. By that time those same people will better understand the leader's basic attitudes and have experienced some of the decisions he or she has made.

Encouraged and guided by several friends and acquaintances who are well versed in the field of politics, I have developed and carried out the "Listening Session" concept twice over the past twenty years. Both were in a parish context; both occurred after I had recently been appointed the church's pastor.

There were twenty-nine sessions at one parish, and thirty-nine at the other. Some 300 people participated at one church, over 400 at the other. I received 700 plus suggestions at the initial parish, 1400 from the second congregation.

We generally gathered at homes from 7:30 to 9:00 P.M. with clusters of six to twenty people. Each participant filled out 3" × 5" index cards, noting her or his name, address, phone number, and place or type of employment. I took Polaroid photos of every group for later posting in a church corridor.

After introductions, the questions I posed were simply these: "I am your new pastor. How can we best serve you? What are the needs of the parish?" They then spoke, and I wrote.

Those sessions give the newly appointed leader a fine opportunity to meet a considerable number of constituents, to catch the general atmosphere among the people, and to hear a host of practical ideas.

Listening sessions like these can set the practical leadership thrust for the first six months and provide raw material for long-range planning to cover the next few years. They also establish the leader as a person, like Gorbachev, who is open, and accessible and who listens.

A Success and a Failure

I recently directed a prayer day for several dozen predominantly lay parish religious education leaders at a nearby retreat center. My two presentations contained some of the remarks about priorities contained in Chapter 3 of this book. They included the suggestions for dealing with those crisis moments created by unexpected visitors or interrupted telephone calls.

Near the day's end I used a brief concluding technique that has proven effective in helping participants focus on a day's experiences and in providing useful feedback for the presenter.

It began with: "We have now spent over four hours together. Shortly you will be returning home. While we hope the day has been good for you, it will have a more powerful impact if you take a moment to identify one idea, one suggestion, one story, or one practical tip that resonated in your heart, that seemed valuable to you, that could be useful over the months ahead in your personal life or pastoral ministry. It will also solidify the day's effectiveness, if you write down that single, worthwhile point."

After a several minute silent interval, I continued: "You can further strengthen the impact of this day by sharing your conclusion with a person next to you. However, there is no obligation to do this at all. You can simply say, 'I pass.'"

A second pause followed, this one a bit longer, for the sharing to take place.

I then concluded: "Finally, you can deepen your own resolve by sharing that one notion with the group. Again, feel no pressure or obligation to do so. All of you may pass on that suggestion, if you wish."

The response was excellent. About a dozen participants expressed in very personal and positive terms the day's particular focal point for them. I simply listened, nodded, and made no comments, except for an occasional and whispered "thank you."

We were now at the agreed-upon closing hour and it seemed necessary to curtail any further responses. However, a hand shot up. The individual posed an objection or question, not a sharing. She did not understand, much less like, the procedure about crisis moments that I had described and illustrated with an example from my recent pastoral ministry.

Here I made a mistake. Instead of listening attentively and playing back for her the objection as I had heard it, with an offer to discuss it afterward, I reacted defensively. I restated the procedures and even allowed some interaction with the others to ensue. Five or ten minutes later I had to refocus the group so we could have the concluding prayer service. I found that the exchange had not been a satisfying experience for anyone.

The positive, calm mood had been broken. The session was now late in concluding and the objector probably felt that she was being attacked. Moreover, I was both distressed by the negative comment and annoyed with myself for not recognizing this to have been a "crisis" moment for the questioner. In addition, I felt dismayed for not responding according to the very procedures I had but moments earlier enunciated to that group. This would have meant a swift and conscious shift to a more listening mode of leading.

My two-hour drive home following this day of prayer was clouded by memories of the concluding event and my poor handling of that situation. I simply forgot or ignored the many successes of the day and concentrated on the failure. Perhaps the next time I will be quicker to recognize that the need in such circumstances is for good listening, not more talking or teaching.

A Quote to Ponder: "The leader must be a superb listener, particularly to those advocating new or different images of the emerging reality. . . . Successful leaders, we have found, are great askers, and they do pay attention."[4]—Warren Bennis and Burt Nanus

A Biblical Role Model: Samuel, visited by the Lord during sleep, finally responded, as the priest Eli recommended, by answering, "Speak, Lord, for your servant is listening."—1 Samuel 3

8

EMPOWERING

One of the gifts of leadership is the ability to spot talent and to help those with talent to develop and display their gifts. The gift may show up on the trombone or the word processor, in accounts receivable or window decoration. The insightful leader provides recognition, support, and guidance, but allows plenty of space and freedom for the gift to flourish and find its own expression. Over his long and very successful career, composer-arranger-conductor Henry Mancini has shown a remarkable ability to encourage and empower others through his strong but "light touch" style of leadership.

Henry Mancini
Composer/Performer/Arranger/Conductor

Quinto Mancini came here from the old country and with an old world frame of mind. Arriving in the United States from Abruzzi, Italy, and eventually settling in the steel town of Aliquippa, Pennsylvania, he brought with him a love of music as well as the highest regard for education and the teaching profession.

An avid flutist himself, it was only natural that he teach his eight-year-old son Henry to play the flute and, four years later, to take up the piano. Mr. Mancini, however, apparently never anticipated that music for young Henry would instantly become not merely a part-time avocation but his consuming passion.

"Even at that early age, music was my overwhelming interest," Mancini says. "I had a passion for it and everything else suffered accordingly. I received only C+ marks in school, perhaps a B-here or there. That was disappointing to my father. He wanted me to go to college and become a teacher."

"Right up to his death some years ago, his message to me was always the same. I remember after winning my third Oscar, he said, 'You should go back to school and learn how to teach.'

"As I said, I had a real passion for music and came to realize later that such a passion for what you are doing is a prerequisite for success in any calling."

During his teenage years, Mancini played in the neighborhood Sons of Italy band and in all the various music ensembles at his high school. He might have moved on to college, but World War II broke out and he was drafted. In the army he was able to continue his playing, but he also began to develop skills in what were his deeper loves—arranging and composing.

After his release from the armed forces in 1946, Henry Mancini joined the Glenn Miller–Tex Beneke Orchestra as its pianist-arranger. This move effectively ended the possibility of formal university training, but provided him instead with rich, informal, and part-time learning experiences. It also gained for him a wife, Ginny O'Connor, a singer in the band, whom he married in 1947.

A few years later, in the 1950s, Mancini began to compose and arrange music for television ("Peter Gunn") and the movies. The rest is history, with an incredible list of successes to his credit, such as *Breakfast at Tiffany's*, for which he wrote "Moon River," and countless awards, nominations, and honors.

A passion for music, study under experts, and hard work have given Henry Mancini recognized success as a world class composer/performer/arranger/conductor. That recognition and those achievements understandably attract other talented and successful artists who want to collaborate with him on different musical enterprises. But there is something more here. Henry Mancini has a unique gift for not only engaging topflight people in cooperative ventures but also for maintaining that collaborative relationship over an extended period of time.

How, for example, have he and movie producer-director Blake Edwards been able to work together for more than thirty years and on more than twenty-five films?

"We both had prior successes and together have done some things which were successful and some which were not so successful," Mancini says. "But we respect each other's talents and get along well with one another. The two of us share a similar dark, black, gallows sense of humor."

In what way has Mancini maintained such a long-term relationship with the musicians who record under his direction?

"Some of my conducting colleagues get nervous and uptight at recording sessions. That makes them rather sharp or harsh with the musicians. The work gets done, but they leave with, you know, a sort of bad taste in their mouth. My approach is a bit different, more low key, although demanding as well. I have tried to be loyal to these very competent musicians over the years although my loyalty may now be getting in the way of a proper performance. Some are older and can't execute as they did in earlier days. I find this a bit hard to deal with."

Is there an approach Mancini employs to bring forth the best efforts of, for example, the Philadelphia Orchestra or the Rochester Philharmonic?

"I am convinced that the audience enjoys soloists—it gives them a greater sense of participation. The orchestra also enjoys having some of their own gifted members featured in a performance. So I prepare a program that includes a good number of solo pieces."

William Cahn, principal percussionist for the Rochester Philharmonic, has benefited from Mancini's approach. During a Summer Music 91 Concert at the Finger Lakes Performing Arts Center, Cahn performed a complex solo xylophone piece. Afterwards, in his typical, respectful style, Mancini acknowledged with applause the rendition and added with a grin, "You played it just as I wrote it."

Cahn observes that Mancini has the automatic respect of

the entire orchestra from the first moment he begins their rehearsal, because of his past outstanding achievements and his totally professional approach. The music is technically and physically well prepared—there are no wasted moments making changes on marked-up sheets of paper. His arrangements are "tremendous, fabulous," Cahn says, "easy to follow." And he displays great respect for the individual players and the total orchestra.

Two young members of the violin section concur. They found that Mancini's rehearsals were extremely efficient, and even finished before the time scheduled. Moreover, these violinists sensed that they were in the presence of a conductor who was definitely in charge and quite demanding, despite his laid-back public persona.

"My style of conducting differs from someone like Bernstein," says Mancini. "Musicians in the orchestras I lead are of superior talent and read music instantly. I like to let them perform on their own as much as possible. When things do start to deteriorate a little, I tighten up a bit.

"Sometimes musicians may get careless and not take the music seriously, especially when it's pop music instead of classical. I've been known in those cases to shout, 'Wake up!' at those who aren't playing properly or giving the music their careful attention."

The violinists remarked that some pop conductors appear to be just "going through the charts," while Henry Mancini treats all the program music with serious respect.

To the audience, Mancini's style as a conductor is personable, humorous, seemingly spontaneous, almost casual. He tends to be very formal with the orchestra in a rehearsal and informal with the patrons during a concert. He conducts with what appears to be a "light touch," with a concluding twirl of the hand here, a lifted finger to end a number there, even leaving the podium during extended solos.

The core musicians who travel with him, the "sidemen" who play drums, trumpet, saxophone, guitar, and bass at each engagement, drew high praise from members of the Rochester orchestra. "He brings such a great band with him that it's a delight for us in the Philharmonic to work with them," one of the local players said. How does he hold on to such gifted performers?

"I need to have these people on whom I can rely totally to do exactly what I want. Their presence gives me confidence that the program will go well. How do I keep them happy? They are professionals—many from I.U. (Indiana University), they have the time, they enjoy playing, they make good money, and they stay in good places. We are the best-fed traveling band in the country."

Most of Mancini's 100-plus albums feature him as composer, artist, and conductor, but recently he has produced three albums with other outstanding performers; the great operatic tenor Luciano Pavarotti, flutist James Galway, and the popular balladeer Johnny Mathis. "I did these because I respect their approach to music and get along well personally with them. I wouldn't do this just for anyone."

Mancini and his wife Ginny have three children, including twin girls (now young women). Is it difficult being the daughter or son of such a famous person? How does he view his leadership role as a parent?

"I fell into a certain syndrome with my son, the oldest child. The time when he felt most need of my presence was just when I was moving from success to success. As a result I wasn't there for him and he got sort of messed up. Now he is forty and has a job with a music company in Los Angeles. Today we talk about what happened then and what we can do about it now.

"My twins, well, you know twins just have each other and the world outside doesn't affect them that much. They both are into music and doing well.

"However, when the kids were growing up, Ginny and I always tried to present a common front. We talked things through. Thus even when I wasn't there, it gave the children, especially the girls, a certain confidence."

Henry Mancini has earned a considerable sum of money through his career in music. But he has shared that with others, funding scholarships and fellowships at places such as the Juilliard School, UCLA, USC, and the American Federation of Music "Congress of Strings." Why? "Stan Kenton, who is dead now, once commented that when the elevator reaches the top floor, you send it back down to the bottom to bring up more people. That really says it all. I really love musicians. They are the best people. Besides, I could be sitting there with the symphony as the second flutist, except for the grace of God."

Henry Mancini's father felt that if his son went back to school and learned to teach, he could really make something out of his life. The sixty-seven-year-old composer, performer, arranger, conductor clearly has done something with his life. But he has also been inspiring and teaching other musicians, even though in a way Quinto Mancini could not have imagined.[1]

Empowering

Henry Mancini has, during a long and distinguished career, been able to locate a host of gifted musicians and engage their services. Moreover, his own light touch leadership style has brought forth the best within them and generated their long term loyalty to him. That, in contemporary terms, is empowerment.

Good leaders do something similar. They identify people's gifts. They tap into their potential. They unleash the possibilities for achievement which dwell within the persons whom they lead. They empower others.

Dustin Hoffman, in a television interview with my brother, described an incident which occurred during the filming of *Midnight Cowboy*. He was very disgruntled at the end of a particular working session because the director had scheduled a rather difficult, highly emotional scene for the late afternoon hours. Hoffman, who had been on the set all day, felt drained and empty, without the high level of energy required to carry out well such a dramatic episode. A perfectionist, and temperamental artist as well, he started to sulk and complain.

His costar, Jon Voight, noticing Hoffman's dark and ugly mood, approached him and asked what was wrong. Hoffman responded with a grumbling explanation of the poor scheduling and of his unwillingness to perform under those conditions.

Voight then reached out, touched Hoffman's arm and remarked, "You are great. You can do it. Now do it!" And he did, in Academy Award-winning style.

Hoffman later observed, "Voight gave me a love tap. He unleashed my potential."

He had empowered him.

Future Projections

Not only identifying people's talents but also projecting their development in the future, especially over any long term period, requires unique skills.

Eddie Kolo does this for a living. For twenty-three years he has been scouting baseball talent, amateurs in schools during the spring and minor league professional players throughout the summer.

What does he look for? Scouts, he says, "try to measure the tangible tools—running, throwing, fielding, hitting, and hitting for power. In a pitcher, you look for a loose arm, a good body build with potential, velocity and movement on his pitches, and skill at throwing pitches."[2]

In evaluating prospective professional athletes does the scout observe more? "A scout has to try to get to know the player in order to assess the intangibles. You want to look at desire, heart, character, and work habits. Usually I try to meet with the kid's guidance counselor or summer league coach. I try to find out the community's impression of the kid."

What are the percentages that, after all this study and analysis, a young ballplayer will make it to the majors?

"It's a crap shoot. You have to project baseball players, unlike basketball or football players. Those guys may be drafted and be impact players the next year. With baseball, most of the players you're drafting are three to five years away from playing in the big leagues. A scout who's used to doing free agent work is going to project how that player is going to be three, four, five years down the road."

Leaders, then, need a certain kind of an observational-intuitive gift or developed skill for this. Such a facility enables them to recognize talents that are present in a person at least in seminal fashion and to predict with some accuracy the blossoming forth in time of those abilities.

In the massive historical novel, *War and Remembrance*, author Herman Wouk attributes such a trait to President Franklin Roosevelt. The book's fictional hero, Victor ("Pug") Henry has just been appointed by his commander-in-chief to an important post for a significant mission.

During the conversation about this assignment, Roosevelt chuckles and says, "Why, that's most of what I do, old fellow. I just sit here, a sort of traffic cop, trying to direct the right men to the right jobs."[3]

Jon Voight served in similar fashion as a leader to Dustin Hoffman during that tense, late afternoon moment. He knew Hoffman was then and there the right man for the right job; he recognized his talents; he understood that Hoffman could and would act out the scene with distinction. He motivated the star to use his gifts; he, in this circumstance, touched Hoffman's future.

A Light Touch Style

As we have seen, Henry Mancini often displays a light touch style of leadership when he conducts a symphony orchestra or directs other musicians at concerts or recording sessions.

The "touch" dimension of that style encompasses those ways by which a leader shows interest and support. They might include, for example, mere presence at functions, letters of commendation, time spent listening to a staff person's concerns, annual or semiannual social events, prayer moments together, and personal notes in their paychecks.

In a large, active organization or office, school, or parish such "touch" tasks, even though quite brief and relatively simple, require considerable time, creativity, and energy on the leader's part.

The "light" dimension of this style means that the leader allows staff persons to breathe, gives them space in which to move and encourages creativity among all employees.

Leaders who admire a light touch style and seek it for themselves have to let go. They cannot control everything and everyone. They won't know each detail, recognize each face, and resolve each issue.

The light touch style of leadership strives constantly to achieve a certain balance between its two dimensions.

Thus, light touch leaders will be there for their people whenever they are needed, but will not be looking over their shoulders at every moment of the day. They will show sincere interest in all events, but will be careful not to intrude, except when it is absolutely necessary.

I have witnessed negative reactions when leaders appear to violate that middle course. In one case, the leader seemingly watched over and wanted to control every detail of people's lives. Many resented this interested, but too tight style and labeled it domination, interference, and intrusion.

In an opposite scenario, another leader allowed enormous freedom and rarely intervened or even commented. Many people complained about this apparent lack of interest, and felt that they were not supported or affirmed by such an open, but too light style of leadership.

The light touch approach tries to follow a centrist path through those extremes.

Leadership in a School System

Secular school system superintendents have very difficult jobs. These leaders often feel "sandwiched" between conflicting pressures or demands from the groups they serve. By the very nature of their positions, such people must respond to boards of education, to employees, to parents, and, in these days, even to students.

For example, several superintendents who are located in the northern part of the United States have told me that the hardest judgments they must frequently make involve the closing of school because of snow or ice storms. They must do so at a predawn hour, after evaluating weather and road conditions. These are absolutely "no-win" choices.

When they decide to close their schools, frustrated and sometimes desperate working parents for whom the school is a kind of free day-care center angrily call their offices in protest. On the other hand, when they decide to remain open despite somewhat stormy weather circumstances, faculty members for various reasons may likewise vehemently complain. No wonder the turnover rate runs high among school superintendents.

I had lunch with one of these superintendents a few years ago. His peers consider him personally to be kind of a maverick. However, they highly respect him professionally and also admire his successful work as an educational leader in a huge, sprawling, and complex school district.

Part of his success can be attributed to a procedure he has established of visiting each classroom of every school twice a year. As any executive knows, that type of management by wandering around requires discipline, the tough asceticism of pushing oneself on a regular basis out of the office and into the field of operations.

Those visits were short, just long enough to get a feel of the class, to establish a more personal connection with the teacher and, in the process, to extend affirming support. An extended stay could have been disruptive and intrusive.

We could label this, too, as the light touch type of leadership.

Micro- and Macro-Managing

Micro-managing and its opposite partner, macro-managing, are words sometimes used today to describe various styles of leadership.

At the outset we need to mention that experts hesitate to employ the terms *manager* or *managing* when referring to leaders. To them, manager or managing smacks of manipulation, of using people, of moving employees around like pieces of machinery, of treating workers as objects rather than persons.

With that reservation kept in mind, however, the phrases macro- and micro-managing do express rather well negative and positive dimensions of the leadership function. Their connections with the light touch style of leading should be obvious.

The Micro-Manager

A majority of department heads at one of our area's massive institutions recently criticized their chief executive officer in the secular press. They accused this leader of being a "micro-manager."

Those disgruntled department heads took a negative view of micro-managing. They judged that their institution's president was excessively intrusive. According to them, this very visible local leader displayed no respect for the expertise of subordinates, constantly interfered with their activities, insisted on making too many minute decisions, and seemed to be always watching over their shoulders. This intrusiveness, they claimed, stifled their initiative, demeaned them, and actually crippled the effective operation of the entire organization.

They felt such strong frustration and intense hostility that these departmental chairpeople, who were highly skilled in their own fields, took the very unusual and highly risky step of airing those grievances in public.

Micro-managing, however, also has its positive side. That type of hands-on, actively involved, "know every detail" style may prove most effective, especially in certain circumstances. Thus when a leader first takes over, when a leader faces an organizational disaster or when a leader must deal with employees who are not good self-starters, opting for the micro-manager approach in those situations may be the wisest choice.

The Macro-Manager

Good macro-managers, on the other hand, practice the principles of subsidiarity. They seek to have decisions made at the lowest level possible within the organization or operation.

Astute macro-managing also empowers others. It identifies real needs and recognizes people's gifts, then merges the two together. By sharing trust in their personnel and allowing them space in which to function freely, macro-managers promote the best utilization of employees' talents.

Nevertheless, the leader who remains too removed, who does

not keep abreast at all of the day-to-day operation, who seldom is seen by employees and never visits with them will eventually run into problems. Confusion, lack of enthusiasm, stagnation, and consequent poor productivity ensue.

Good leaders manage by frequently walking around, by listening attentively, by praising people often, by saying little, but thinking a lot and by carefully making only major decisions.

The best leaders are sometimes micro- and sometimes macro-managers, depending upon the situations before them.

Tapping Talent

Henry Mancini's style of leadership brings forth the best within the musicians whom he directs. But this famous composer and arranger also has an ability to locate gifted artists and persuade them, through various means, to work with him.

How in similar fashion do pastors of parishes tap into the enormous talent before them? How do they empower these people? How do they identify their gifts and unleash their potential? How do staffs working with them accomplish those things as well? How do both working together develop practical and successful methods of motivating individuals to volunteer their time and talent for building a better church and a better world?

Pastors may empower parishioners in, among others, these six ways:

1. They can create an open climate and display a positive attitude that welcomes, in a general way, active involvement of members in the life of the parish. By their preaching, teaching and organizing, pastors communicate not only their willingness, but more, their strong desire that every person somehow share her or his gifts in at least one worship and service activity.

2. They can directly invite individuals to share particular talents for a particular project or organization. Thus, to illustrate, although within the Catholic church we currently witness an explosion of lay ministries, still the personal invitation of the pastor or parish priest continues to be powerfully effective.

Contemporary books on leadership stress the intangible, but important factor of top management giving attention to individuals in an organization. The pastor asking a specific person to undertake some specific task is but an example of that principle in practice.

In the novel *War and Remembrance* cited earlier, President Roosevelt, even though he was pressured from every side and preoccupied by countless matters, took time to chat with "an anonymous midget of a naval captain and made him feel important to the war."

"Pug" Henry, the naval officer, impressed by this remarkable attention given him, still reflected that it was, after all, his own "way with a ship's crew; he tried to give every sailor a sense that he mattered to the ship."[4]

Pastors in similar fashion ideally try to make every member of their flock feel important to the parish and to communicate a notion that each one matters.

3. They can facilitate a weekend, usually in the early fall, dedicated as Volunteer Sunday, Stewardship Sunday, or Time and Talent Sunday.

At all the worship services, the pastor speaks briefly on some theme that connects the day's biblical texts with the concept of sharing gifts or serving others. The preacher then turns this theological reflection into practical action by inviting each parishioner to pick up a pencil and the form placed beforehand in the pews. The form may list as many as 100 activities and opportunities for service, with every age group represented.

During the remainder of the homily time, the speaker moves through this form, gives an explanatory description here and there, and encourages people to sign up for tasks that seem suitable and appealing to them.

4. They can sponsor an appreciation dinner or event for volunteers, most often in the late spring as parish activities tend to wind down.

5. They can allow other people to shine and receive applause.

6. They can seek to inculcate and foster a similar spirit of empowerment within their staff personnel.

Staff members can empower parishioners in much the same way as the pastor does, following many of those steps noted previously. But they do so in the areas of their particular expertise and with obvious adaptations.

Our first ever Summer Vacation Bible School serves as an encouraging case in point. The religious education coordinator who was responsible for this program sought through printed announcements and personal contacts children, teachers, and assistants for the week-long morning event. Within a few weeks she had assembled a capacity crowd of students (133), an ample number of adult teachers (24), and a remarkable group of young people as helpers (20).

This positive response actually was no surprise. The coordinator has been practicing an empowering style of leadership for several years now. She taps talent, organizes the personnel, gives them guidance, and lets them go. Afterward she allows those others to take the bows, an important characteristic of any leader who empowers.

A survey of reportedly dynamic Roman Catholic parishes across the country identified several common ingredients in those nearly 100 faith communities. One characteristic centered around the possibility for the active involvement of people in the life of the parish. So many and varied activities were available for volunteer participation in those lively churches that if members had the desire, they could easily become involved.

In each of those enthusiastic, alive, and exciting churches one will most likely find a pastor and a staff who, like Henry Mancini, have both a gift for identifying talents among parishioners and a style of leadership that unleashes the potential which they have discovered.

A Quote to Ponder: "'Leadership' connotes unleashing energy, building, freeing and growing."[5]—Tom Peters and Nancy Austin.

A Biblical Role Model: Mary, the mother of Jesus, noted the embarrassing lack of sufficient wine at the wedding feast of Cana. She brought this to her son's attention, but he declined at first to do anything about it. Undaunted, she simply told the waiters, "Do whatever he tells you." Christ obviously changed his mind, used his power, and transformed the water into excellent wine.—John 2

9

AFFIRMING

Helping others to identify their gifts and put them into practice is a vitally important task for leaders in our very complicated world. But that is only the beginning. What is hardly less important is encouraging and sustaining those individuals the leader has set in motion, reaffirming the leaders' confidence in them and their confidence in themselves. Leaders may be reaffirming the work of an individual or of an entire staff. The reaffirmation is sometimes as simple as a word or a note, sometimes it's an event for the whole group.

Sister Charla Commins, C.S.J.
Woman Religious, Social Worker, Executive Director
of a Catholic Charities Agency

In 1962, after completing twelve years in Catholic schools, Susan Commins entered the Sisters of St. Joseph. Her first years in the convent were typical for those days. She followed a regimen of careful formation and strict discipline during Postulancy and Novitiate. Then, after receiving a full black and white habit, the young woman professed vows of poverty, chastity, and obedience. Susan adopted a derivative of her father's name, Charles, to be her name in religious life.

The choice of name suggests a strong parental influence in her young life, and Sister Charla agrees.

"As I reflect back," she said in an interview, "my mother was a social worker before I knew what the term meant. There was always somebody staying temporarily at our house, or a family she was helping, or people in need who received some groceries and a little cash from us."

"My father taught me how to laugh and how to treat all people equally. Despite the fact he was a relatively highly placed executive for the P & C food company, he spoke with the same smile, tone, and friendliness to the truck drivers and warehouse personnel as he did to the corporation vice president."

"They were constantly giving to my two sisters and to me, but it was very clear that their relationship with each other was their top priority. That relationship and that priority lasted for more than fifty years, until my mother's death."

Her undergraduate and graduate studies at the College of St. Rose in Albany, New York prepared Sister Charla for eight years as a teacher of English at several area parochial schools.

She divided her summers in those years between taking more graduate studies and doing volunteer work in the GAP ("Growth and Progress") program, a creative effort to identify and form leaders among primarily black young people in the city of Albany. At that time she met and collaborated with a youthful "street" priest named Howard Hubbard who, not many years later, became bishop of the diocese.

"Those experiences," Sister Charla recalls, "opened my eyes to a whole new reality. I had never been deeply hurt in my life. My parents were caring. We were not affluent, but led comfortable lives. I had not been abused, knew little about alcoholism and less about the truly poor or disadvantaged. What we tried to do and could accomplish with those youth simply whetted my appetite for that type of ministry."

Her close friend and colleague, Sister Lauren Van Dermark, unknown to Sister Charla, was undergoing a similar transformation. They both enjoyed teaching, both sensed their positive impact on the students, and they both acknowledged the value of religious sisters as teachers. But they both began to wonder if the Lord was calling them to shift their efforts to the social service field.

As often happens at such moments, other developments unfolded and opened a door for these two young nuns. The leaders of Catholic Charities in the Albany diocese, who recognized a need to expand their efforts, decided to create an affiliated human service office in Saratoga County, New York, the home of the famous city of "health, horses and history."

The challenge of launching the new facility fell to Sisters Charla and Lauren. Relatively inexperienced as they were, in 1975 they began their pioneering, full-time, hands-on labors in behalf of people in need. Sister Lauren concentrated on the elderly, Sister Charla on adolescents and families.

The hours were long and the caseloads seemingly endless. Sisters Charla and Lauren quickly realized they needed to sharpen their skills and expertise in these new fields. They gave over their evenings after work and their Saturdays to study for their Master of Social Work degrees at the State University of New York in Albany.

The Saratoga Springs agency continued to grow. Eventually Sister Charla added an additional responsibility to her already busy counseling tasks by accepting the position of associate director. In 1989, she became full-time executive director of the agency.

As the leader of a staff that includes fifty-two full time people plus nine affiliated practitioners, Sister Charla describes her central role in this way:

"I envision my primary function as one who affirms the gifts or talents of our staff people, who supports them in their often very difficult work. These are professionals, but they deal with domestic violence, rape, addictions, abject poverty, dysfunctional families—real hard stuff. I try to be there for them."

Sister Charla has now been a member of the Sisters of St. Joseph for more than a quarter of a century. Like many or most women religious, she discarded the black and white habit about two decades ago in favor of simple but conservative street clothes. Only seeing a small cross or hearing someone address her as "Sister" would alert unknowing strangers to the fact that the agency's executive director belongs to a religious community. But the faith in God, love for the church, and concern for those in any need, which she inherited and learned from her parents, are as strong as ever.

Today those qualities of faith, love, and concern for others are behind the direction and especially the support she provides for her corps of colleagues at Saratoga Springs. What are some of the ways Sister Charla accomplishes this?

• By often expressing a "thank you" for tasks accomplished;

• By trying to show a sensitivity to the personal stresses and problems in the lives of her staff—a death or critical illness or some other serious family situation;

• By making sure when a project or event receives publicity, it is the staff person immediately involved who is mentioned and not herself.

Despite her self-effacing attempts, the local community has recognized Sister Charla's leadership abilities. The Soroptimist International of Saratoga County, for example, honored her with its 1992 Women Helping Women Award.

The honor noted that the human services agency which she directs "serves more than 11,000 residents of all ages. Charla was one of the original members of the Domestic Violence task force. She is cochairwoman of the AIDS task force for Saratoga County. She has been involved in the Saratoga County Teen Pregnancy Coalition, the College of Saint Rose board of trustees, the Shelter of Saratoga Coalition for the Homeless, and the Albany Diocesan Directors Advisory Council."

Barbara Lombardo, managing editor of the *Saratogian*, in her coverage of the award event described meeting Sister Charla: "I'm embarrassed to say I didn't know Sister Charla, and expected someone weighted down by the burden of serving the county's needy. Instead, up stands a young, fit woman who could be an understudy nun on the Father Dowling show, full of pep and humor. I think she's happier as head of Saratoga County's Catholic Family and Community Services."

Such accolades haven't halted Sister Charla's creative measures to affirm staff members. The following are some additional steps she takes to provide that kind of support:

• By taking time to send individualized Christmas cards and to dash off frequent notes of praise;

• By offering department heads some cash to take their staffs out for lunch when the unit is undergoing a particularly stressful experience;

• By encouraging workers during less pressured summer months to enjoy the more leisurely pace as a time to fill up their reservoirs of energy for the hectic demands soon to come;

• By organizing a retreat day in the fall and a fun day in the spring to bond more closely together the large, diversified, and geographically scattered staff.

Sister Charla Commins summarized the main thrust of her efforts to affirm as an executive in this way:

"My goal would be to step aside and let staff take the bows when things are going well and to be there and accept responsibility when events turn out badly."[1]

Giving Compliments

This dedicated nun and competent social service executive has found practical ways of supporting staff that both fit her personality and seem to work. Another word for such support giving is affirmation.

Passing on praise to others is a major component of the affirmation process. As we have seen, learning how to take or accept compliments helps strengthen one's self-image. Conversely, being able to give compliments well helps us bolster the self-esteem of others.

Complimenting another may appear to be an obviously easy task. And it certainly is less delicate and less difficult than correcting others. But even in this instance leaders can learn how to do things a little better.

A key notion is that the compliments must be honest and authentic. The good sense suggestions that are given later in this section will prove counterproductive if they don't flow from a good heart. My brother who has twenty-five years of experience in a leadership role to back up his point says that "most people have built-in baloney detectors and will sniff out the false praise in a big hurry."

Another essential concept is that the compliments must flow from the leader quite naturally and not be, or at least seem, contrived or artificial. Slavishly observing the recommendations that follow will usually result in this real or perceived artificiality.

With those cautions in mind, I would like to offer some practical tips for effectively passing on praise to others that have helped me. They did not come from a textbook on Christian ethics or a manual on Catholic spirituality. Rather they appear in essence on the pages of *In Search of Excellence: Lessons from America's Best Run Companies.*[2] In the managerial world they are called positive reinforcement techniques. They seem to work for businesses; perhaps they can work for other organizations such as churches as well.

1. *Give the compliment immediately.*
When a person achieves a certain goal, receives some public recognition, or does an outstanding piece of work, let that person know you know it—and quickly. Drop her or him a note, make a phone call or stop by in person.

Thomas Watson, Sr., the principal founder of IBM, practiced a form of "wandering around" management leadership. He constantly walked through company offices and production facilities, observing people at work and asking questions. When Watson spotted a particularly impressive activity or received a useful suggestion, he stopped, wrote a check right on the spot, and handed it over to the employee. It was a very specific form of praise.

Compliments are welcome any time. But when the good deed and the good word happen in quick one-two succession, the praise has an added zest.

2. *Be specific.*

Nice job, great dinner, good sermon, fine talk, beautiful outfit, attractive presentation, interesting class—we all enjoy hearing comments like these. But when the compliment is more specific, the glow lasts longer, the pleasure goes deeper, and the compliment—for being more detailed—rings even truer.

When you want to make the praise more specific, it makes good sense to pay close attention to what the other person is saying or doing. For example:

Preaching the homily at the funeral of a priest is a special challenge. We are speaking before our peers—usually an unsettling experience. I like to send a note complimenting the preacher afterward and I want to be specific in my comments. That means I must listen to the homily with particular care.

3. *Look for reasons to give a compliment.*

Management experts have discovered that attainable goals motivate people far more effectively than nearly impossible objectives. In other words, the possibility of being successful may well encourage me to work harder. On the other hand, if the goal seems hopelessly beyond reach, requiring the next best thing to a miracle, I'm likely to give only a halfhearted effort from the start.

Wise leaders thus try to develop structures, policies, and attitudes that invite success. They try to create situations in which people are likely to succeed. The leaders are then in a position to give frequent compliments for jobs well done.

4. *Remember that praise from a leader means much to the receiver.*

Have you ever seen a framed congratulatory letter from the president of the United States on the wall of one's home?

Have you heard a commendatory telegram from a governor read at some testimonial dinner?

Have you received a note of praise from the CEO of the mega corporation for which you work?

In all probability neither the president nor the governor nor the CEO knew personally the family in that home, the individual being honored, or the employee of the company. With our technological expertise of photocopying, those leaders may not have even actually signed the letter.

It makes no difference. The words of praise have a basis in truth—as the recipient knows—and there is a warm satisfaction in the gesture. The wisest leader tries to make the congratulatory message as personal and nonroutine as possible.

Although the praise of a leader does have a unique impact, some people today take a fundamentally different approach. They instead seek to develop a style and a method by which leaders foster self-praise or self-congratulation in others. That promotes a sense of autonomy rather than of dependence. This demands a unique mind-set on the leader's part and will require that he or she acquire certain new and deft skills, but the goal is both intriguing and clearly valuable.

5. *Reward good performances in tangible ways.*
A raise or bonus is the obvious and perhaps ordinary method by which leaders acknowledge a task that is well done. However, both large and small institutions have discovered that nonmonetary rewards—"hoopla" one author terms them—will likewise warm people's hearts and lift up their spirits.[3]

Stanley Coyne has been using creative hoopla to motivate his employees for years, probably long before the idea or term ever appeared in a text on management.

In 1929, he began his first full-time job after completing school—working in a gas station. Coyne soon discovered that most laundries would not accept the grease-and-oil-soaked rags used by car mechanics and pump attendants. Recognizing a need and a market, he quickly located a neighborhood laundry that was willing to handle the soiled items. Coyne and the laundry entered into a partnership which lasted for some years.

During the six decades since that beginning in the Depression, Coyne has built the operation into Coyne Textile Services, a multimillion dollar, international corporation. Over the years he has hired a number of topflight executives to help run the massive business.

How has he hung on to these really competent personnel? "By never forgetting any employee," Coyne says, "and by rewarding them with incentives like new titles or a better parking spot in the company lot." In other words, he has used creative "hoopla" as well as cash bonuses to reward excellent performance.[4]

6. *Give compliments frequently, but irregularly.*
When the giver is constantly giving out compliments, they come to be expected and taken for granted.

Surprising and unexpected expressions of praise at irregular intervals are more effective.

This requires extra thoughtfulness on the part of the compliment giver.

Every two weeks, after signing the church employees' paychecks, I often also enclose in the envelope a brief, personal note—just a few lines—on some colorful, motivational cards. Occasionally I get some nice feedback and I certainly try to make the words individualized and heartfelt. But I don't always include the notes because I don't want them to become routine on my part or seem perfunctory to our employees.

Building Up the Staff

Sister Charla's affirmations encourage the individual men and women who work with and for her. But some of her other efforts are directed toward the staff as a whole at the social service agency.

A very important function of any leader is to do something similar—to raise staff morale by creative ways that are effective.

We have a terrific group of part-time and full-time employees at our parish. Their ages vary greatly, from Beth, who just obtained her first working papers to Mary who finally retired because of poor health around her eighty-ninth birthday.

Obviously these employees also have widely varied educational backgrounds, professional training, and life experiences.

Beth, for example, like most of her contemporaries, is computer friendly. She recently sent me a multicolored thank-you note that was obviously produced on the family's or her own word processor.

Mary, on the other hand, was terrified of the computer. That did not matter. The charm of her personality and the wisdom of her many years made this remarkably energetic woman a fine receptionist.

The staff members have distinctive and varied jobs to do, which reflect a remarkable diversity of their aptitudes. These include administration, religious education, music, liturgy, youth work, social service, housekeeping, maintenance—and all the roles that constitute the functioning of a large and active organization.

When you have so many individuals with distinct talents carrying out so many diverse activities, there is real potential for misunderstanding and conflict. Only if everybody works toward agreed goals and keeps the channel of good communication open can the risk of large and small explosions be minimized.

Prudent leaders start and maintain the kind of staff meetings that keep communication lines open. My experience has shown me the need for several kinds of gatherings:

• *The regular and routine staff meeting*

These sessions deal with the nuts and bolts items of everyday operations. They give everyone on the staff opportunities to discuss what is happening in their fields; they are a chance to work out scheduling conflicts that invariably arise; they give everyone the opportunity to discuss common concerns.

Some church or parish staffs meet weekly or biweekly. After a year or so, our people decided that a monthly 10:30–12:30 morning session was sufficient. Holding meetings too frequently can become a needless drain on staff members' time and energies. Too few meetings, however, can lead to conflicts and misunderstandings.

A substantial prayer and educational section at every staff gathering helps to create an atmosphere of cooperation and free communication.

• *A yearly or semiannual staff planning session*

There are really two kinds of these planning sessions. The more practical get-together sets up the calendar for the next six months or the school year. The other, more philosophical session, looks back and ahead in rather general terms. How has the year been? What are some of the parish needs? Where should we be going during the immediate and distant future?

Both of these meetings are best held at an "away from the

parish", setting where there will be no interruptions. Moreover, they require a solid block of time, like an entire day or two days. That way the staff can contemplate the issues at a leisurely pace that inspires creativity and long-range thinking.

• *An occasional prayer day*

To step aside at an out-of-the-way place for a day of prayer and reflection once, or better twice, a year does wonders for the staff and, not least, is an inspirational model for the whole parish.

There should be no business items, no agenda; no problem solving. Simply to be present with the Lord and to one another in the Lord. A couple of brief talks on spiritual matters, several periods for quiet meditation, and perhaps some moments for shared prayer and prayerful sharing, all at a retreat house or similar setting.

Serving, as we do, 1500 households or some 6000 souls can be demanding and exhausting. These prayer days help keep us focused and motivated.

• *Several recreational events each year*

These can be a supper or a show, a lunch or a concert, a picnic or a party.

In our case, the pastor treats all of the staff, with their spouses or significant others, twice each year—around the winter holiday time and during the summer months. We usually have dinner together and some kind of entertainment.

In addition, our full-time personnel are treated to lunch every other month to celebrate birthdays that occur within that time.

Working, praying, *and* playing together aids in building and strengthening bonds among staff members.

• *Growth days*

These are normally all day sessions in the fall and the spring designed to develop the personal and professional skills of staff members. Some "outside expert" generally guides those days that may touch upon subjects such as good communication techniques and procedures for managing conflicts.

Discouragement, it seems, comes easily these days both to individuals and to groups working together. The world's woes appear oppressive and discouraging. But honest and effective encouragement and support—affirmation—for a staff can help immeasurably to counteract the negativism. Leaders who can provide that kind of encouragement will surely have happier and more productive associates. This is one of the goals Sister Charla Commins pursues at her social service agency in Saratoga County.

A Quote to Ponder: "You may be disappointed if you fail, but you are doomed if you don't try."[5]—Beverly Sills

A Biblical Role Model: Elizabeth was swift to praise her pregnant cousin Mary when the mother of Jesus came for a helping visit. And she did so in very specific terms.—Luke 1

10

EVALUATING OTHERS— AND YOURSELF

The most difficult, sensitive, and often the most painful aspect of the leader's role is having to offer criticisms and corrections to associates, but also (and not least) having to take a hard and possibly corrective look at one's own performance. The need is great for both objectivity and sensitivity, firmness and compassion, tact and directness.

Some of the leaders interviewed in this book are national figures, whereas others are well known only in their special fields. Kathleen Bernardi, on the other hand, is best known within her relatively limited church and community circles where she is active. She is no less a leader, but her leadership role is essentially as a full-time wife and mother. Yet in that role Kathleen, too, finds that she often has to evaluate herself and others, to correct herself and to correct and be corrected by others (even as a CEO might feel the corrective hand of his shareholders). The business of evaluation is not easy, either for Kathleen or a CEO.

Kathleen Bernardi
Wife, Mother, Volunteer

Kathleen Bernardi's father, Tom Phillips, grew up in a relatively large (4 children) Italian family that was generally stable, affectionate, and secure.

Kathy's mother, Beverly, unfortunately, had an almost op-

posite growing up experience. Beverly's mother died when
she was seven and her younger brother was two. Their father tried to raise them, but it was more than he could
handle. The two children were sent to live, sometimes together, sometimes separately, with relatives and friends.
Then, when Beverly was fourteen, her father died and the
children were taken in by a kindly lady, Helen Nappa.

Beverly felt then and feels now deeply grateful for what
this woman did, especially in reuniting an orphaned teenage girl and her brother. She eventually, despite the awkwardness, came to call Helen Nappa, "Mom." Kathy, in
turn, has thus always and quite naturally spoken of her as
"Grandma Nappa."

Tom and Beverly married in 1955. They lived in a rented
apartment, and began putting aside money from their two
jobs for a down payment on a house. Kathleen was born
about a year after their marriage. Four years later, when
they had their second child, Beverly stopped work to stay at
home until their two daughters reached an older age.

When she was ten, Kathleen experienced what she terms
"a weird year in our life." Her dad and her uncle, apparently weary of northern winters, sold their houses, packed
their household goods on rented trucks, and took off with
their families for Florida. It was uncharacteristic of her father and in time proved to be an unwise venture.

"I remember the tears," Kathy recalls. "I went around
our neighborhood and said good-bye to those who lived
nearby and to our family members. We cried half the way
to Florida. But then there was the excitement of the move,
and since our two families—my uncle also has two girls—
were together, we had some support for one another.

"They had rented two houses only a few blocks from each
other in Hollywood. But, these homes were really nowhere
as nice as ours back home and kind of run down. However,
our parents evaluated the situation and decided to clean up
the houses. The very adventure of doing that, day after day,
took away some of the sadness. My mother and aunt are so
fanatic about a home being clean and orderly that we
worked hard trying to repair and clean the houses."

The two brothers found jobs as salesmen. Nevertheless,

several months later they left the deteriorated Hollywood houses for different positions and adjoining apartments in Fort Lauderdale.

"This was another adventure," Kathy says. "Before I had a house with a yard. Now we were in this small apartment and I was sharing a room with my sister. We were scrunched up. We had to walk to school. There again we all stuck together—the four cousins—because life is a lot faster there. And we felt like country bumpkins. The textbooks were a year behind, but the kids in other ways were two years ahead. A lot of the time I was afraid. I didn't really like these kids. I felt threatened.

"My mother got a job and each day at the end of school we prayed that one of our fathers would be waiting to pick us up. But if not, we would walk home—once more the four of us taking care of each other. We would then lock ourselves in the apartment until our parents returned."

Kathy can't recall a specific time or incident when both sets of parents decided that the move to Florida was ill-advised. But after a year the four adults evaluated the situation. They concluded that they didn't want to bring up their children in that environment and realized that their families back home up north meant too much to them.

The Phillips returned to the Syracuse suburb of Camillus and Kathleen entered the large, sprawling West Genesee school system. During her teenage years, she made a mistake one day. She vividly remembers the way her parents responded.

"My father didn't exactly rule with an iron hand," Kathy declares, "but he clearly taught us right from wrong and laid down the rules. My mother tended to be a little softer about things. They both were very involved in all our activities.

"We lived next to the high school, and one afternoon my girlfriend came home with me and two boys joined her. They were just there, nothing else, when my father walked into the house from work. He just flew off the handle and he said, 'You've got to get my permission,' and some other things. I was devastated.

"When my mother came home from work later, she said

to me 'Did your father find out what they were doing?' I
was crying and sobbed 'No, he didn't even bother to find
out. He just kicked everybody out. How can I show my face
again?'"

Kathy's mother turned to her dad and questioned him,
"Do you trust her?" He nodded affirmatively. "Then find
out."

That element of mutual trust and respect typified by this
incident governed Kathy's relationship with her parents
throughout high school. There were no inflexible curfews.
As long as dad and mom knew where she was and with
whom, they showed confidence in her and gave their daughter considerable freedom. Part of that was a reaction on her
mother's part to the rigid curfews with regular groundings
for violations, however trivial, that she had known under
her own foster mother.

"But," Kathy comments, "I never took advantage of that.
I never wanted to violate this trust and we really had no
major problems during my high school days."

After graduation, Kathleen Phillips went on to college for
secretarial science. She obtained a position with the Niagara
Mohawk Power Corporation, and continued to date, in on-
and-off again fashion, Archie Bernardi, a sweetheart who
went back to her high school days. Archie completed his
undergraduate work at Syracuse University and joined Niagara Mohawk, the local power company, after working five
years as an engineer at Chrysler Corporation. Following
their marriage in 1978, Kathy and Archie had a daughter
Jamie in 1982 and a son Daniel in 1986.

Like so many contemporary mothers, Kathy went
through an agonizing evaluation event when her first child
was born. Her career seemed very important to her, and
day care, she says, was not very popular then. Consequently,
Kathy placed an advertisement for a baby-sitter; a fine older
woman subsequently replied. This sitter was quite willing to
cook and clean, as well as care for the infant Jamie. But
Kathy wouldn't let her—she insisted that she simply watch
over the baby. Since the company had no part-time arrangements, it meant that Kathy would leave for work at 7:30

A.M. and return at 5:30 P.M. She thus hardly had a thing to do with Jamie.

"After two weeks of this," Kathy recalls, "I sat down with Archie and said, 'For me it is either a full-time career or motherhood. This is ridiculous. Someone else is raising my child.' This woman was truly wonderful with Jamie, but I felt one of the parents should be there for the first few years. I put in my notice and stayed on another six to eight weeks. I don't regret it at all. I don't look back. To me there was no question about it."

Kathy sees herself as a rather emotional person who likes people and enjoys doing things. Archie, on the other hand, she perceives as a much calmer individual. He tends to be more private in regard to his personal life. Those personality differences naturally have caused some difficulties. In recent days, however, Kathy has come to realize that before you can hope to change others, you first need to change yourself, understand yourself better. That new self-knowledge has helped Kathy to understand Archie better and has strengthened their relationship.

How about raising and correcting her own children?

"I look back on what my mother did for me. I'm thirty-six years old now, but my mother is still my best friend. We can talk for an hour on the phone about anything and I trust her completely. She left many things up to me when I was growing up. She trusted me. I try to do the same with Jamie and Dan.

"Archie and I complement one another. He is more laid back, and lets the kids do things. I tend to do them myself, to be in more control.

"I try," Kathy continued, "to teach them to have great respect for people and things. To put themselves in the place of someone else who is hurting or being attacked by others. It seems to be working, for I hear stories of Jamie coming to someone's defense in school.

"We don't belittle the kids when we correct them. When they have done something wrong, I try to hold back a little before immediately correcting them because I tend to get more excited and emotional. Archie, on the other hand, stays calmer. We believe the kids can better understand the point you want to make if it is done when things have calmed down."

There is, Kathy admits, a curious reversal when one of the kids gets hurt. Archie then becomes excited and emotional, but she thinks, as her mother once explained to her, that is because men are hurting inside for their children in such a situation. Kathy in that context generally does not fly off the handle, as would be her custom, and works to be the calming influence. The kids are hurting enough, scared enough, she believes. They need love right then and there. Before any questions are asked.

"We try also," Kathy says, "to be honest and open with the two children. I let them see my moods. They see us fighting and making up. I apologize when I make a mistake.

"Archie and I try never to discipline them in a mean way or without being flexible. For example, Danny loves to have stories read to him. One night he was watching television and had his trucks scattered all over the room. We told him several times to pick them up, but he kept glued to the screen and paid no attention. We felt that it was necessary to discipline him because of his attitude. We sent him up to his room, which is our form of punishment in our house, being separated from the family.

"After awhile we could hear some noise upstairs and it was clear he had not gone into his room. When I checked, he was sitting at the top of the stairs. We know that he is afraid to be upstairs by himself and that was why, frightened, he sat on the step.

"Instead of insisting that he go into his room, we adjusted the punishment because he had suffered enough already."

Many young Catholics stop regular churchgoing for a period after they graduate from high school. Archie and Kathy were a part of that trend. Kathy made her way back first. She began going to Mass regularly and took a refresher course in Catholicism. Now she teaches religion to sixth graders each week, spends an hour every Wednesday from 10:00 to 11:00 P.M. in prayer at our Perpetual Adoration Chapel, and helps with the classes for adults who seek to enter the Catholic church.

Archie never objected to her return, but felt no need himself to be at church each week. Kathy didn't push her husband or lecture him much on this, but as so often happens, the children got to him. In this case, daughter Jamie's persistent wish that they worship as a family touched his heart. Now Archie is there regularly, even by himself on some Sundays, and finds religious matters interesting. The parish has become an important aspect of his life.

Kathy is likewise evaluating her own future. The children are moving along. Is it the moment to resume her career at work? Or is the attraction she currently feels toward education, school, a different degree, and a quite different profession a sign from God for her? The answers to those questions will emerge in time as she follows her own inner evaluation process.[1]

Evaluating Yourself

Kathy Bernardi experienced a significant, but unscientific evaluation event while she growing up. The ill-starred move to Florida and the subsequent decision to return north involved many persons making a series of decisions. Later in adulthood as a married woman and new mother Kathy went through her own evaluation process. Do I return to work or stay at home with Jamie? She decided to move in one direction, but then almost immediately reevaluated the situation and reversed her decision.

Family and personal evaluating experiences are part of everyone's life, however unconscious the process may be. But today almost all organizations large or small conduct evaluations. Still "evaluation" and "evaluating" are high-risk words.

If we mention to employees the term *evaluation*, announce the start of an evaluation process, or hand out the forms for each individual's evaluation, we observe an instant rise in the anxiety level of some staff personnel.

The strong human tendency to overemphasize our negative

side and dwell on mistakes rather than reflect upon successes makes the evaluating procedure for some a dreaded experience. Such people fear the prospect of being criticized by their supervisor or employer. No one, of course, particularly enjoys hearing about weaknesses and failures. Persons who are inclined to exaggerate flaws thus even more expect the evaluation process to be for the most part an unpleasant event, a lengthy and painful examination of all that they did wrong since the last review.

Others, however, are more confident about their own abilities and performances, where still aware of their shortcomings. They may welcome evaluations as opportunities for affirmation of what they have done and occasions for personal growth.

Regardless of their pleasant or unpleasant nature, their dreaded or welcomed status, annual, semiannual, or periodic evaluations have become standard operating policy today.

For example, pastors of parishes in our diocese undergo a fairly complex evaluating procedure after six years in office. Diocesan personnel annually work through some type of an evaluation process. My own parish staff complete their evaluations each June in time for the salary adjustments made at the start of the fiscal year on July 1.

Both secular and religious organizations often use forms for evaluation that list points such as attendance, punctuality, reliability, initiative, productivity, and compatibility. Check-off boxes are placed next to each item marked "excellent, above average, satisfactory or needs improvement." In addition, these forms usually contain several more general, open-ended sections: For example, "Overall Evaluation," "Supervisor's Comments," "Any Aspects Producing Satisfaction or Dissatisfaction."

Employee and reviewer complete the form separately, then discuss the response, and, finally, together sign a revised document.

Our parish staff used a similar form during my first year as a pastor and found it somewhat mechanical or artificial and less than satisfying. The next June our business affairs manager created a different form, shared the draft document with lead staff members, made the changes that they recommended, and then distributed copies to the thirty plus employees.

These questions make up the essence of that document:

1. What do you like about your work?
2. What don't you like about your work?
3. What should be done to change dislikes to likes?
4. What are your strengths?
5. What are your weaknesses?
6. Describe your goals and expectations for the last year.
7. Were you satisfied with the results and experiences of last year?
8. Do you believe you have been appropriately informed and instructed to do your work or to achieve these goals?
9. If not, how can this be improved?
10. What are your dreams, visions, goals, and expectations for the coming year?

Those questions effectively motivated each employee to conduct her or his own constructive, healthy self-evaluation. The reviewer then needed only to listen, to echo the highlights presented, to offer a few observations, and to reinforce the person's goals and expectations for the coming year.

How well do periodic evaluations work? How helpful are they to individuals and to organizations?

One veteran executive with some years experience of evaluating others and, in turn, being evaluated sees little to be gained by this experience. He says, "The process was hated by those who inherited only praise, and it succeeded mostly in reminding us all that we were part of a large and essentially soulless corporation which regarded us as expendable pieces on a giant checkerboard. That is now and will forever be the net result of the evaluation process."

I did not detect that degree of animosity among our own parish staff during and after the first year's evaluation process. They appeared to be open to, or even welcomed, the opportunity for an evaluation of their performance. I did feel uncomfortable with the rather mechanical and mathematical check-off form described previously. When we reviewed that year's evaluation procedure, the staff, too, indicated their displeasure, or at least, their dissatisfaction, with it.

There was near universal praise of the next year's experience with the new form—for several reasons:

First, they themselves endorsed the importance or value of the evaluation process, however painful or time-consuming it may be.

Second, they critiqued, revised, and eventually approved the series of questions, thereby making them their own.

Finally, they discovered that this particular procedure was more of a self-evaluation project, which forced them to focus upon themselves rather than to await divinely inspired observations from their supervisor or reviewer. They tended to spend considerable time privately reflecting on the past year and writing out their answers to the questions. The later, generally hour-long discussion with the reviewer further clarified and strengthened their own insights.

In the second year we used the ten-question process, and the feedback seemed quite positive. The staff did, however, gently suggest that the interview with their pastor—this writer—was much more effective when he was relatively alert and his eyes were not drooping as he listened to their responses.

Confronting Others

Giving compliments is a necessary, but relatively easy and generally satisfying task for leaders. Confronting others is likewise a sometimes necessary, but a much more difficult and often painful process.

Parents and teachers, priests and bishops, physicians and supervisors, presidents and executives—all in leadership roles on occasion face the uncomfortable challenge of confronting persons for whom they are responsible.

Sometimes the encounter goes well; frequently, however, the experience leaves both persons involved with bruised feelings.

Three friends and colleagues of mine, two priests and a nun, each remarked on separate occasions that confronting, constructively criticizing, or correcting others—call it what you will—is the most difficult thing that they do as leaders. As long-time pastors in parishes and as a school principal or teacher for thirty years, the three of them have had many experiences in this area.

My brother comments that "giving criticism, even the most

constructive, as parent, volunteer, pastor, or assembly-line boss, is the most dangerous and sensitive thing a leader does, because it is fraught with counterproductivity and long-term damage outweighing any short-term benefits."

Confrontation is risky because, in my brother's words, the mentor or leader "needs first to look into her or his own soul and be sure that the criticism is entirely just, and won't backfire in hostility."

Some 1500 years earlier St. Benedict in his written set of rules offered similar suggestions for the leader of a monastery. He cautioned the abbot to hate sin and to love the brothers. "And even in his corrections, let him act with prudence, and not go too fast, lest while he seeks too eagerly to scrape off the rust, the vessel be broken. Let him keep his own frailty ever before his eyes, and remember that the bruised reed must not be broken."[2]

Confrontation is also risky because the leader generally does not know what lies behind or underneath the behavior that needs to be confronted.

One of my brother's favorite assistants, a junior critic, began coming to work late, being late with copy, even dozing off at her desk. It was uncharacteristic of her and Chuck asked her if anything was wrong. She just said she felt tired all the time and apologized. My brother told her to take time off if she needed it. She didn't, but shortly thereafter the cause of the weariness appeared—she was being consumed by unfelt and undetected cancer and died in a matter of weeks.

My brother is still haunted by the thought that instead of asking he might have criticized, instead of inquiring he might have complained, instead of first seeking to understand he might have immediately confronted his delinquent critic.

Confrontation is also risky because if the leader or mentor does *not* confront or make the necessary constructive criticism, the inappropriate or problematic behavior can become a morale problem or a source of resentment to others.

Our rectory doubles as a home for three clergy and a set of offices that is frequented by many. For several good reasons the doors need to be locked at all times. Our custodians recently began to leave the back door unlocked because of the inconvenience involved since they are in and out of the building so often.

One day a stranger, having come in by the back door, simply appeared unannounced at the office of a staff person and startled her. There was no harm done, but it underscored the need to have every door locked at all times. It was for me to correct, confront, or criticize the custodians about the matter. They took it well and, after my explanation, recognized the necessity for the measure despite the inconvenience for them.

It would have been risky and unwise for me to ignore the problem and to avoid the confrontation. That would eventually have caused more serious morale and operational difficulties.

Kathy Bernardi, through the story of her growing-up days, as well as the account of her current role as spouse and parent, has modeled some appropriate "confronting," "correcting," and "criticizing" attitudes and approaches.

Here are a few further suggestions that may help minimize the pain and maximize the profit to be gained from confrontations which a leader judges necessary to make.

Expect some resistance and negative reaction.
Not many of us welcome constructive criticism or enjoy hostile letters. Few people appreciate being told that they are wrong or that they have executed a task poorly.

St. Dorotheus, an abbot of centuries ago, maintained that those who find fault with themselves accept all troubles cheerfully. These would include misfortune, loss, disgrace, dishonor, and every other kind of adversity. We presumably can add corrections or criticisms to that list.

According to the abbot, people with this frame of mind simply believe that they are deserving of such things; as a result nothing can disturb them. No one, in that monk's view, could be more at peace than people who so fault themselves. I have found few, if any people who so fault themselves.

The late Anthony DeMello put the same idea in more contemporary and earthy terms. If we consider ourselves truly as asses, he maintains, then it won't bother us when others say that we are wrong or stupid. After all, he says, what do you expect from an ass? I have found few people who honestly call themselves asses.

Generally the leader who confronts can expect from the one

being confronted, at least initially, overt anger, hostile counter-attacks, sullen resentment, or silent withdrawals.

Beware, all those uninvited.
This flows rather naturally from the previous suggestion.

Most of us seemingly resist confrontation and react negatively to criticism from our supervisors, employers, or others in similar positions who have the authority and responsibility to do this. How much more will we reject the unsolicited critical comments, for example, of a friend or colleague?

When you offer uninvited or unauthorized negative remarks about another's appearance, words or actions, be prepared for a blast back.

"You didn't ask me, but I wanted to offer you a little friendly criticism about your recent. . . ."

"You are right! I didn't ask for your opinion!"

In an uninvited and naive step years ago, I penned a mildly critical note to a well-known national figure. The instant, succinct reply advised, "In the unlikely event I would ever seek your opinion or advice, I will contact you. Until then, I suggest you mind your own business."

My annoyed correspondent signed the letter, "Cordially yours in Christ."

Respond immediately.
The further we move beyond an incident which needs confrontation, the less effective will be the leader's criticisms.

There is a parallel here with the process of giving compliments. Praise presented when the deed done dwells fresh in the mind of the person involved will seem much more authentic and will affirm the individual more powerfully.

So, too, if we do not confront a person relatively soon following the behavior in need of confrontation, it normally would be better to drop the matter.

Just do it.
When someone hurts or annoys us, when a person performs poorly or acts irresponsibly, we usually feel troubled and distanced from the individual who has done this.

Not to surface and deal with the issue will drive the negative sentiments deeper within, eventually to emerge in more destructive fashion. Moreover, a definite gap between ourselves and the other will continue until the time a certain confronting and reconciliation occur.

So just doing the correcting is desirable, even if we do it imperfectly.

Pick the proper time and place.
Criticizing another is a delicate procedure under the best of circumstances. Doing so at inopportune times or in unsuitable situations increases the risk that the encounter will go badly for both the one confronting and the one being confronted. Thus, criticisms should *never* be made:

On the fly. Such a rushed exchange minimizes the importance of the correction and maximizes the danger of a misconnection. It also has a certain demeaning impact upon the one receiving the corrective comments.

At low energy moments. Friday afternoons, late in the day, just before vacations, following lengthy work sessions, after intense and enervating labors—all are occasions when both parties are weary, drained, and not at their best. Tempers flare faster on those occasions and feelings bruise easier.

In front of others. The confronted person suffers needless embarrassment in that circumstance and, preoccupied with this humiliation, will very likely miss the real point of the criticism.

Concentrate on current concerns, don't resurrect ancient mistakes.
When necessary criticisms are, unfortunately, suppressed or postponed, there is a tendency to surface all these unaddressed matters much later when an exchange about another matter occurs. That overloads the confrontation process and almost surely guarantees its failure.

The only exception here deals with the formal warning procedures of an organization. In this case, the leader may need to bring forth an earlier written and signed correction document for discussion.

Use a rifle, not a shotgun approach.
We normally can handle only one or two specific criticisms at a

time. Attempting to cover more than that during a given session will usually be ineffective.

Address actions or behavior, rather than an individual's attitudes or personhood.
Human beings can judge only external deeds, not inner intentions. God alone fully knows the human heart.

Moreover, while external actions naturally mirror interior attitudes, there is not an automatic evident link between the two. Any poor behavior may proceed from a wide variety of motives. Finally, because we rightly confront an individual's inappropriate acts, it does not mean that we thereby are devaluating the person's intrinsic worth.

Follow some established methods of confronting others.
Communication skills experts have designed simple, but sound methods for problem solving, conflict management, and personal confrontation. Although they look easier on paper than they actually translate in practice, the principles nevertheless are helpful.

John Lawyer and Neil Katz, in their *Communication Skills for Ministry,* for example, chart the barometer of emotions involved in an assertion or confrontation.[3] They also explain the necessity for good listening skills to execute a mutually satisfying confrontive encounter.

The asserting person will need to make the confronting statement several times. After each occasion he or she immediately must listen down the other's raised emotional level in order for the message to penetrate. Ideally, at the conclusion, the asserting leader has made the necessary confrontation and the corrected individual has truly heard the criticism, yet feels valued as a person.

Blanchard and Johnson, in another approach, describe in the best-selling *The One Minute Manager,* a "one minute reprimand."[4]

According to their scenario, the leader or mentor reprimands people immediately and specifically, clearly indicating what the person did wrong. The leader then tells the other how he or she feels about this mistake and pauses in silence long enough to let the other feel how the asserter feels about the problem behavior.

The leader shifts gears at that point and shakes hands or touches the confronted person in a supportive way. The leader at the same moment underscores the individual's value and praises other past efforts, but not the performance in this situation. Finally, Blanchard and Johnson stress that when the reprimand is over, it is over.

Good advice for anyone correcting another: When it is over, it is over. Time for both to move on.

Persons with healthy self-esteems do better at giving and accepting criticisms. They are able to be assertive when necessary, but not in an aggressive manner that wounds the individual being confronted. Moreover, they do not passively allow others to hurt them, suppressing their anger or resentment, only later to explode with an inappropriate attacking outburst.

The unconditional love that Kathy Bernardi received as a child and which she now seeks to bestow upon her children builds that type of self-esteem. This in turn means that the confronting and evaluating which goes on in their home, as it necessarily goes on in every home and every life, will more likely be constructive rather than destructive.

A Quote to Ponder: "There are only two people who can tell you the truth about yourself—an enemy who has lost his temper and a friend who loves you dearly."[5]—Antisthenes, the Cynic Philosopher

A Biblical Role Model: John the Baptist fearlessly confronted a leader of the land, losing his head and his life because of this criticism. He also turned admirers from himself to Christ, indicating that Jesus was the one they should follow, that Jesus was the long expected one.—Matthew 14; John 1

11

EXCELLENCE

When you think of it, the leader is probably a leader because of a commitment to excellence. It's an elusive characteristic, a deep-seated motivation. But good leaders have recognized the quest for excellence in themselves, and part of their goal as leaders is to communicate it to those whom they lead.

The talented corporation executive Tom Wyman was encouraged from an early age to excel, to make the most of his many gifts. He responded positively to the encouragement from his parents and from his first mentors in the business world. He has displayed his dedication to excellence through four illustrious decades in the corporate world and through his considerable volunteer work in education.

Thomas Wyman
Corporate Executive

Tom Wyman came into this world during the Great Depression days of the 1930s, born of well-educated, but financially strapped parents. His father, an Amherst alumnus, suffered with spinal meningitis at a time when medical experts knew little about the disease and less about its cure. His mother, a Smith alumna, thus struggled to provide for the education of their three daughters and the younger boy. The children knew from the start that scholarships were the only path to college and part-time jobs the only source of extra cash.

At the age of thirteen, Wyman forged his father's signature on a letter to Phillips Academy at Andover, Massachusetts. In it, Wyman requested an interview with the recruiter from this topflight New England prep school during his scheduled visit to the Wymans' home city of St. Louis. Later in the early summer a letter arrived at the Wyman house announcing that Andover had not only accepted Tom as a student for the fall but had granted him a full scholarship. Since no one in the family had known anything about the application, the discussion that followed the letter must have been interesting.

Wyman's first months at Andover were not outstanding. "I was very small, quite short as a matter of fact, and hadn't grown up yet in many ways. I failed two courses in the first semester. I was in well over my head."

But toward the end of the year an event and a new acquaintance were to touch his future profoundly. Bill Pugh, a classmate from Youngstown, Ohio, who was athletic, organized, disciplined, quite mature—a big man on campus, and well respected by his peers—asked Tom if he would care to room with him in the fall. "It didn't take me long to say 'yes.' But I kept wondering why this topflight person would want me as a roommate."

Pugh obviously detected qualities in this classmate from St. Louis that he admired, qualities which the then insecure Tom Wyman didn't recognize within himself. That invitation, his appreciation of Wyman's gifts, and their companionship over the next three years helped change Tom's life. He sprouted physically; he matured emotionally. Naturally brilliant, Tom also responded well intellectually to Andover's challenging environment. He emerged as a school leader and graduated with honors in academics and athletics.

Whereas most Phillips Academy alumni favor Harvard, Princeton, or Yale, Wyman selected Amherst for various reasons, not least that it was his father's alma mater. "At Andover I'd learned how to study, how to write, and even how to talk a little bit. With the Andover background I thought it would be easy to excel at Amherst. But this was after World War II and there were a good number of veterans at the school, very grown up men and quite serious about their education. Amherst reacted accordingly with greater demands on its students and it turned out to be a continuing challenge to me."

During those early college days, Wyman once spoke with his mother about athletics and their important role in life. Since he was doing well in team golf and soccer, he wondered whether the constant emphasis on academics was the best preparation for the future.

"Sports are a part of life," his mother told him, "but you are there to get an education. You can always play games, but this is the only opportunity you will have to become educated. I want you to do something for me. For me the Phi Beta Kappa Key has always been a symbol of excellence in education, a sign of real achievement. Try to earn one for yourself."

He did, graduating magna cum laude with a B.A. in English from Amherst in 1951.

His career since then, after two years of Army service in Korea, has been almost entirely in the corporate business world. Most notable or at least most publicly known would be his tenure as chief executive officer and chairman of the board for CBS during the 1980s until he resigned in 1986 following a takeover of the network. He has also been on the boards of an impressive number of major corporations and, before CBS, he was president or chief executive officer of several large national or international companies. Recently he has returned to full-time work in a very different field, as chairman and chief executive officer of the S.G. Warburg Co., a British investment banking firm.

Two experiences proved particularly powerful in terms of Tom's own continued personal growth.

After working a few years for the Nestlé Company at its U.S. headquarters in White Plains, New York, Wyman was sent by that firm for a year of graduate study at IMEDE in Lausanne, Switzerland—the management development institute sponsored jointly by Nestlé, the Harvard Business School, and the University of Lausanne.

"I was the only American among the forty-two there," Wyman recalls, "and consequently became instantly globalized. But the core studies were almost all about American companies, and as a result it was easy for me to excel."

Toward the end of that year, while Wyman was still in his early thirties, the chairman of Nestlé's approached him, and speaking in heavily accented English said, "Wyman, I want to talk to you about what you are going to do next. Do you think you could give up eating cheeseburgers and learn to live and work as a European?"

With some hesitation, Wyman asked what specifically the chairman had in mind.

"I am not going to give you a job description," the chairman said, "I am offering you a chance to grow and get bigger!"

Wyman accepted.

The first day in his new post, the chairman gave him a challenging directive:

"I am very serious about this language business. You had a little French in school. I have two things to say to you. First, this is our last conversation in English. Second, here is your new secretary—a very competent woman who speaks only German, Italian, Spanish, and, of course, French."

Wyman spent countless nights suffering headaches from a day's intense concentration of trying to reflect and communicate in French. One morning, four months later, his secretary remarked: "Mr. Wyman, I think the time has come for me to confess that I do speak English."

After a number of satisfying years with the Nestlé Company, Wyman returned to the United States and began working for the Polaroid Corporation. European companies, he judged, took better care of their employees than American firms. But U.S. corporations, it seemed to him, had increasing sensitivity to issues beyond their own interests, such as having a concern for the poor, sharing wealth with others, and promoting education on a global level. He wanted to be involved with that thrust of corporate efforts and joined Polaroid to do so.

It was there that Wyman experienced a second memorable, personally growth-producing period in his life. Working with Polaroid's founder and president, Dr. Edwin Land, put Wyman in intimate daily contact with a visionary, exciting and creative leader.

"He sometimes would phone me around 10:30 at night," Wyman remembers, "and say, 'Tom, could you come right over. I just received some new material from our lab and it has all kinds of possibilities for us.' I'd look down at my pajamas, reluctantly change and go to his office.

"There Dr. Land would greet me at the door with 'Oh, Tom, I apologize. I had just eaten and thought it was 3:30 when I called you. After I hung up my lab assistant reminded me it was nearly 11:00 P.M. But now that you're here. . . .'"

As we will see, Dr. Land also possessed a keen appreciation of international matters and an exceptional ability to deal wisely with a potentially explosive challenge that Polaroid faced in that area.

Tom Wyman has hardly been inactive since he left CBS. From his twelfth-floor New York City office in the Olympia Building, he carries on as a trustee of Amherst College, the Ford Foundation, and the Aspen Institute. In addition, he serves on the board of an English company that is currently introducing some innovative methods to promote their workers' volunteer efforts on behalf of the local community. The corporation offers matching grants not only for financial donations but also for time contributions. Employees, for example, may teach three hours a week in local schools on company time and receive their normal pay for that time.

In effect, Tom Wyman today is seeking to make it possible for young people, especially those suffering economic hardships, to excel, particularly in education, as he did with help and guidance at Andover, Amherst, and elsewhere forty to fifty years ago. And presumably he will pursue these objectives in his new role at S.G. Warburg.[1]

A Commitment to Quality

While he was a student at Phillips Academy, Wyman spent the summer months with his grandmother at Auburn in upstate

New York. He worked with the grounds crew at a local country club, earning spending money for the year ahead and improving his own game in the off-hours.

Several miles from Auburn is the lake and village of Skaneateles, both of which bear a remarkably close resemblance to the idyllic setting of the film *On Golden Pond*.

The clear, clean waters of Lake Skaneateles are perfect for swimming, sailing, and water skiing. The surrounding hills with their attractive farms and the many expensive homes along the shore make a daily evening dinner cruise and a mail boat luncheon trip popular summer attractions.

Far from Switzerland and the towers of Manhattan, one Skaneateles businessman shares that same commitment to excellence that has been such a strong component of Tom Wyman's life. And the villagers enjoy the oddly endearing rewards.

Doug's Fish Fry stands right in the center of Skaneateles' small shopping district. It's an extremely popular spot, but its folksiness seems in sharp contrast to the artful sophistication of other businesses.

Red signs with white printed lettering scattered around the restaurant set forth the philosophy and the operating procedures of Doug's highly successful place.

One sign proclaims:
"Doug's has No
Waitresses
Reservations
Credit Cards
Coffee
There's no reason for it. There's no rule—it's just our policy."
Another says:
"There is nothing worse than receiving bad service and then having to tip 15%–20% for it!
"So, at Doug's we have no service, no waitresses and no tipping."

The policies probably help—and certainly don't hurt—Doug's business. People come in great numbers to enjoy his fried fish, hot dogs, ice cream and soda, milk or beer. Mocking McDonald's, Doug has his own tally board which at last count declared that 1,273,000 fish have been fried there since April 1982.

There are four reasons why Doug's draws such crowds: quality food, friendly service, affordable prices, and a refreshing philosophy.

Those were Doug's goals when he launched his business. "We will work hard to give you quality, fresh, good tasting food served in a clean, friendly atmosphere," he announced. "We offer decent portions at fair prices." He works hard to sustain the ideals he set for himself.

"We buy fresh fish direct from the fish piers in Boston and Gloucester. It is trucked to us on crushed ice *FIVE* times a week (not once or twice).

"Our milk shakes are made with hard ice cream, real milk, flavor syrup, and malt. We never use a premade soft mush mix at Doug's Fish Fry."

Many of Doug's customers have been with him since he opened and they have nothing but praise for the friendly service. Friendly service begins with cheerful employees, and Doug does a lot to build staff morale and thus inspire their loyalty.

New employees (blue shirts) can eventually be elected to the workers' board of directors (red shirts) by their colleagues if they live up to the restaurant's standards of hard work, friendliness, and loyalty.

"Doug cares about us," one of his long-time workers says. "He often asks our advice; we are like family here."

"If you like something about this place," another sign says, "tell two friends. If there is something you don't like—tell Doug."

A sign on the suggestion box says, "I will see every one of them and I care. Thank you. Doug."

A local newspaper review of Doug's Fish Fry summed it up: "Portions are gigantic, the service fast and the prices rock-bottom."

Doug's Skaneateles place is a casual, down-to-earth, and inexpensive restaurant, but smart shoppers have also figured out that there is nothing casual about the quality and value of the food. Excellence is where you find it.

Rising Above Mediocrity

In 1969 Polaroid discovered that its cameras were being used in South Africa to make photos of individuals for the passbooks so hated by the black and colored residents of this country. Polaroid's total business in South Africa was rather small. But the matter of the passport pictures had a global impact. Pickets protested before the New England offices of the corporation, demanding that the company withdraw from South Africa. Dr. Land, in a wise and sensitive move, decided that the decision as to whether or not to withdraw Polaroid's investment in that country should be made by the local employees (25 percent of whom were black) in their Massachusetts plant, not by the management board of directors in a distant city.

To gather firsthand information, he sent Tom Wyman and three black workers to South Africa on a fact-finding mission. Upon their return they made appropriate recommendations for the company, which included the publication of a full-page statement in the *New York Times* decrying conditions in that racially divided country.

Ten years after Wyman's journey, I was invited to lecture for four weeks throughout South Africa at the Theological Winter Schools sponsored by the resident Catholic bishops.

Each week a partner and I would speak from Monday through Friday to audiences of about 125, mostly clergy, some nuns, and a few laypersons. On the free weekends we visited and worshiped with the residents of different "black" or "colored" townships scattered across this troubled apartheid-divided land.

One Saturday night outside of Durban we dined with a distinguished, dedicated black pastor and several of his parishioners, including two young women who were gifted ballet dancers.

During our conversation the pastor bemoaned the absence of commitment to excellence among his flock because of the social conditions.

"My people have grown comfortable with mediocrity," he said. "In this land they know a black or colored person can never achieve the top rank or the first position. They can never become chief executives. White persons must always occupy those posts.

"These young women, for example, would never be admitted to the Cape Town Ballet, even though their talents might be superior to other, white performers."

Despite his complaint about this enormous obstacle—the contentment with mediocrity—that pastor had somehow inspired the parishioners to create excellence in their worship.

When we concelebrated Mass with him over the weekend, for example, everything was of superior quality: music, vestments, sacred vessels, readers, servers, and the people's participation.

Motivating to Excel

How did this leader inspire those burdened people to set their sights on excellence?

His personal love for the liturgy would be one powerful motivating factor. His own commitment to serve as the best possible presider at their worship services would be another. His repeated exhortations to the congregation, his emphasis on the dignity of the Mass, his practical training sessions for lead participants such as readers or musicians, and his willingness to provide quality worship materials such as vestments and vessels, would be still other inspirational forces stirring within parishioners a desire to excel in whatever they did at or for the church.

How does any leader motivate her or his followers to excel? Here are a few suggestions that have been found to be successful in a variety of organizations.

By example. Actions speak louder than words. A leader who works hard, who is always seeking to grow, improve, and learn better methods of doing things influences others without saying a single thing.

Tom Wyman was obviously influenced by his close contact with Dr. Land of Polaroid and the chairman of Nestlé. They inspired him to make the best possible use of his inborn talents and his rich training. "When you are with interesting, exciting people like that," Wyman says, "if you want to have their support, you must do things that make you needed, worthwhile, valuable to them. You reach down for the best within you."

By presence. There is great value in a light touch leadership that gives others ample space to develop their own creativity in an atmosphere of independence. Nevertheless, the regular and visible presence in the workplace of leaders known for their commitment to excellence does bring forth the best in those who work with them.

The contemporary idea of management "by walking around," which includes an insatiable curiosity and a good deal of wandering through the workplace—as practiced by IBM's Thomas J. Watson, leaves no doubt what a good idea it is.[2]

By setting high standards. Taking over a new job, commencing a new project, or beginning a new year, the leader has a good opportunity to establish goals. These had best be few in number and easy to understand.

Ray Kroc, the late founder of the McDonald's hamburger chain, set goals that were simplicity itself. He wanted the shops to be sparkling clean all day, every day, and the service to be consistently efficient and friendly.[3] These goals are clear, if not always easy to achieve. If the goals can be said catchily and often, so much the better. McDonald's, for example, has made a kind of litany out of the letters Q.S.C.& V.—Quality, Service, Cleanliness, and Value.[4]

After all, how did that South African priest inspire his people to a commitment to excellence? He could offer them no financial incentives, only praise for their superior accomplishments—and reminders about how good their own excellence made them feel.

Urging with Caution

When Mrs. Wyman urged her son to earn a Phi Beta Kappa key, it was clear that she knew that such an achievement was within his grasp. The parental genes were in place, or, in Wyman's words, "some celestial authority" bestows such gifts or talents. "The challenge," he says, "is to make sure we use well the resources given us."

For him, not to graduate magna cum laude or to become a member of Phi Beta Kappa would have been a failure to utilize his God-given abilities.

But Phi Beta Kappa is not a goal every student can realistically shoot for. For leaders, but parents especially, to set unrealistic goals can backfire, and lead to frustration, disappointment, or even tragedy for the achievers. Vince Lombardi to the contrary notwithstanding, not everyone can win—that is, be Number One, or graduate summa or cum laude. What matters is knowing you have made the most of your talents. The wise leader does not demand more or less—than a colleague's best efforts.

Gary Clark is an outstanding wide receiver for the Washington Redskins football team. His coach, Joe Gibbs, says of him, "He's one of the greatest competitors I've ever been around. His spirit is unique."

The short, talented, and hard-driving athlete says, "I want to end up number one when I'm finished playing. I don't like being anything but first . . . I'm going to play until I'm number one. That's always been my goal. I want to be the best in everything I have done."

This determination makes Clark push himself and also to explode when his teammates don't produce perfectly. Where did this intensely competitive spirit come from?

The star attributes his anger (mellowing a bit after seven years in the National Football League) to his determination and his determination to his upbringing. His parents emphasized excellence and didn't tolerate mistakes.[5]

But what if he doesn't achieve number one status, or does, but later someone surpasses him? Will he feel that his life is a failure? Will he become discouraged and see himself devalued as a person? Since no one is perfect in this life, how well can he deal with imperfections, faults, and mistakes? Clark will one day, if he has not already, have to confront those realities.

Competition can push us to reach down for more and to tap the very bottom of our reserve. That's as it should be. But a cautionary note is required here. The army advertisement says it well: "Be all you can be." In other words, be your best and be contented regardless of how that plays out in comparison with others.

Tom Wyman over the years has concluded that the measure of whether a particular school or job or responsibility is right for an individual rests in the question: "Can I make a difference and will it make a difference in me?" If the answer is yes, then the chances are that such a school, job, or responsibility is likely to be worth choosing, because it will bring out the best in you.

A Quote to Ponder: "Perfection is not an accident."—Exterior factory wall advertisement, Eagle Motors, New York City

A Biblical Role Model: Peter immediately answered Christ's call to follow him and, later, acknowledged that he had left all things to walk in Jesus' footsteps. There never was any question about the intensity of this man's generous love nor did he ever hesitate to utter idealistic promises, even though human weakness caused him often to fall short of his goals.—Matthew 4; Mark 10

12

ON BEING A SERVANT

The leader, in a real as well as a philosophical sense, is also a servant, drawn to leadership by the hope of being of value to others in some way and on some scale (to raise a child, teach a class, create jobs, steer a multinational corporation, or conduct a symphony). Leaders cannot help revealing themselves, or their inner qualities. Ideally those include humility, hope, and joy. Those are the qualities we want to find in our leaders, although there are others (arrogance, insensitivity) that we can gladly do without. But above all, we hope to discover in our leaders an unselfish willingness to serve.

For three decades, Pam Keller has shown those positive qualities of leadership around the home, at church, and in the work place.

Pamela Keller Panebianco
Housewife, Mother, Family Life Instructor

Pamela Keller showed in her earliest years that she would become a woman of strong determination, religious faith, and dedicated service. Her parents had no formal church affiliation. They did not take Pam to Sunday worship and they never insisted that she go on her own. But some devout friends and neighbors encouraged the little girl and she responded by attending services every week. In 1965, when she was thirteen, Pamela decided to be baptized in the tiny

Methodist church at Upsons Corners, a rural hamlet of Oswego County in upstate New York.

During her high school days she continued to go to church regularly, sang in the choir, and taught Sunday school. Later Pam shifted her affiliation to another Protestant denomination and, when she was eighteen and a college student, she became an elder of the Presbyterian Church. During those days she took a comparative religion course at the State University of New York in Oswego, a class that sparked her interest in Catholicism and later led her to enter the Catholic church.

She completed college, earning a Bachelor of Science degree in education as a teaching major with special concentration in history and social studies.

"I intended to teach," Keller says, "but those were days when teaching jobs were scarce. During the summers I had worked as an intern for Oswego County Social Services. My mentor recommended that I be kept on that fall after graduation as a full-time employee. Since I had some sociology and social work courses at college, I was able to take a civil service examination and they hired me as a caseworker.

"I worked for Family Services, so I was dealing with all kinds of domestic problems—housing, jobs, tensions with children. Later they asked me to shift my attention to older clients since the movement toward gerontology was just beginning.

"I met Mike around that time," Keller remembers, "and since he was Catholic I decided to find out more about the church. I have always said that if the church had not gone through the changes of the Second Vatican Council, I would not have converted. I was looking for a church where you could be very involved and take an active part in Sunday worship. The church gave me that opportunity in the Mass."

Her beau, Michael Panebianco, had been married before and divorced, although the church had granted him an annulment. Nevertheless, he had, through no fault of his own, lost contact with his two sons from that marriage. Pam was surprised when she learned all this, but it never became a big issue for her. It did, however, worry her mother who feared that carrying such heavy baggage into a marriage could threaten its future success.

"We were married on Thanksgiving weekend, 1976. I continued as a caseworker while Mike was selling hydraulic and pneumatic equipment throughout New York State.

"After a few months," Pamela explained, "we became concerned about birth control. We didn't want children right away for two big reasons. Mike and I wanted to get used to being husband and wife first of all without any children. Furthermore, I had never been away from home and so that was a big adjustment. Then there was also the question of Mike's children. They had been a large part of his life and we expected them to become part of ours, but we didn't know where they were or when they would, if ever, join us.

"I talked to my doctor about the pill. I had thought it was the most reliable method available and was taking it. But he explained the possible side effects and that I couldn't take it continuously throughout my marriage. He recommended also that after five years I stop for awhile and that I needed to plan ahead for my children.

"I thought that there has to be something better than this and something approved by the church. We called our priest, invited him to dinner, and hit him with the rough, heavy question of birth control. He connected us with a doctor and his wife who were instructing others in Natural Family Planning."

Mike and Pam followed this lead, paying for and attending three classes, and then sitting through another series of three sessions. Learning and practicing Natural Family Planning (NFP) was a frightening experience for them at the start. There was a lot riding on this, they said, so they both needed to learn the method right and do it right. Moreover, they were, respectively, twenty-eight and twenty-four, whereas the other couples at the training classes tended to be older persons who had their children and simply wanted to have no more. In addition, Pam had been on the pill for those first months of marriage and needed to stop taking them in order to begin charting her cycles.

They both felt sad and annoyed that no one had told them about NFP during the marriage preparation process that included an Engaged Encounter Weekend. This sadness and irritation sowed the idea within them of becoming NFP instructors, a notion that was strongly encouraged by their own mentors. However, they needed to spend a year using this method simply to accomplish the learning, charting, and adjusting that was necessary.

By then the pressure to avoid having a child was not so great. But, following the NFP system, they still postponed pregnancy for three more years. At the same time Mike and Pam began to teach the method to others. Because of their relatively young age, they became very credible witnesses to its practicality, value, and reliability.

The Panebiancos decided to have a child about four years after their marriage and reversed the process, using NFP to produce or pinpoint a pregnancy rather than to postpone or avoid one. Her doctor was quite surprised when, armed with charts and figures, she announced to him that she was pregnant. And she was.

Around this time, they moved into their own house in a Syracuse suburb where she continued on as a caseworker, although she later taught social studies in a Catholic high school. Both of them kept up as NFP instructors, and Pamela also became the part-time director of the area's Natural Family Planning office. She likewise, for reasons she doesn't even know today, volunteered to serve as director of the Confirmation class at their local parish.

"Those were very stress-filled, even though satisfying days," Pam remembers. "I breast fed our first child for a year and a half. We had to be very careful and cautious then. That takes a lot of trust in the Lord and understanding upon the part of the husband. The baby also demanded so much time and energy that there wasn't much of either left over for intimacy with my husband. We also found out that my mother had cancer.

"Several years later we decided to have another child, again reversed the process, and I conceived. Unfortunately,

I had a miscarriage, but soon became pregnant once more and bore our second boy, Phillip.

"After he was born we had decided to limit our family to two even though we had hoped for a girl. But as time went by our desire for a daughter increased to the point where we decided to plan another pregnancy. In our teaching we like to relate this story to point out that NFP allowed us the freedom to change our minds about the size of our family. We hadn't chosen a sterilization procedure that would have closed the door on our fertility and we would never have had our beautiful daughter, Petrina.

"What discourages us with teaching NFP is that there seems so little support from the clergy, doctors, and others."

Although the lack of support causes some discouragement for the Panebiancos, it has not dampened their enthusiasm for NFP or their willingness to serve the Church in these and other ways. Now forty-four and thirty-nine, respectively they are able by their age, experience, example, and words to relate the value of NFP to issues such as the deepening of marital intimacy, the matter of sterilization, the religious training of children, the promotion of a healthy attitude toward human sexuality, and the fostering of good parenting skills. They instruct couples in their home, give talks on the subject before various groups, and appear on several videotapes explaining NFP. In addition, Pam also serves as a eucharistic minister in their parish.

"We are a small voice in a big world," Pam remarks, "but this task is bigger than we are. It is God's doing."[1]

Serving Others

A common thread or theme runs through Pam Panebianco's life: service to others. Caseworker for a county social service agency, teacher in a Catholic school, instructor or guide in Natural Family Planning for couples, caregiver to her dying mother, coordinator of Confirmation class, parent of three, spouse—all of these require, at least ideally, a basic willingness to serve other people. Some would call that servant leadership.

For Christians, Jesus both teaches and models this type of servant leader. "Love one another as I have loved you." "No one has greater love than this, to lay down one's life for one's friends." "The Son of Man did not come to be served, but to serve, and give his life as a ransom for many."[2]

Contemporary examples abound of people who espouse the concept of servant leadership and live it out in quite different ways.

• Jack Ryan, the central character of Tom Clancy's remarkable novels, serves his country in lengthy and intriguing episodes. On many occasions, he risks his life either to save England's royalty from terrorists or to stamp out international drug traffic or to avoid a worldwide nuclear holocaust.

In one of the later stories, Ryan reflects on what governmental leadership entails. He says, "There are always those who're smart enough to know that the power that comes with government service is an illusion. The duty that comes along with it is always greater in magnitude."[3]

• Tom White is personnel manager or, in current terms, director of human resources at the Sherwin-Williams paint plant in Richmond, Kentucky, a short distance from Lexington. The factory does not function according to today's increasingly popular "self-managing work teams" approach. But company officials do view that system as the ideal and are aiming for this goal through a "team spirit" or "team concept" system of operation.

White is responsible for 250 permanent and 20 temporary or seasonal employees. His main task is to train the many teams of four workers each who produce the plant's product—coatings for automobiles. All four team members know how to execute the four different kinds of tasks their team performs, from carrying on purely manual actions to directing relatively sophisticated computer controls. They rotate these jobs among themselves every one, two, or three months as the team itself chooses.

Each team has a leader, something akin to a foreman of former days. White, who was once a union shop official, trains new team leaders or retrains veteran ones. He stresses that they are not "bosses," but coaches. Their main thrust is to facilitate others on the team making decisions, like how often to rotate the various jobs.

Listening to others and teaching others how to listen to one another is Tom White's primary service function as human resource director. He finds himself using those same skills when he returns home at night and serves as father to his four children.

• Dan Roche, now fifty-three, has held service positions in religious organizations throughout most of his adult life. The jobs have included being a teacher at Catholic schools in the United States and a community organizer for almost a dozen years in the Far East. Today he directs the Family Life Office for the archdiocese of Cincinnati. This post essentially means serving others by, for example, putting on marriage preparation programs for the engaged, helping the separated and divorced, or assisting the clergy with family life projects. His battered VW contains boxes of books, booklets, and handouts destined for the latest upcoming workshop or conference.

His wife, Laurie, is an award-winning reporter for the *Cincinnati Post*. Each weekday morning at 6:30 she leaves their home for the newspaper office, returning in early afternoon so she can be with her three children, all under ten, and two under five—and prepare their supper. Dan takes care of breakfast for their son and two daughters.

Both are leaders in highly professional fields. But the service called for in their positions as director and journalist wanes when compared with their responsibilities as parents. The marked-up calendar on the refrigerator door speaks volumes about this point—flute lesson here, soccer game there ("our car pool"), school meeting at another place.

In the midst of such a pace, chicken pox descended upon the household, with itching and painful red sores covering the two little girls' faces and arms. Getting up three times in the middle of the night to comfort a crying child hardly leaves one fresh for a day of Family Life Office decisions or pressure-packed newspaper reporting.

Servant leadership means, as the word suggests, serving others. Such service requires a giving of self, an unselfishness, a forsaking of our own desires that we may fulfill the needs and wishes of another. It has many forms, not the least of which are the ongoing, but hidden and mundane duties of parenting.

• Parish priests, hearing the telephone ring in the middle of the night, know that usually means an emergency sick call.

When the phone rang in my room one evening at 12:45 A.M., I had been asleep for about thirty minutes, just long enough to be stunned and foggy as I stumbled from bed to desk and picked up the receiver.

A husband's voice from the local hospital said, "Sorry to bother you at this hour, Father, but Mother has had some bad spells. It looks like we will lose her tonight. Could you come up?"

"Of course. I will be there as soon as possible."

My lips uttered those words more out of duty than compassion. My head and heart knew what to do, but my tired body groaned.

The day before had been long and tiresome. Since our schedule called for me to offer the 6:30 Mass the next morning, I already was looking at a short night. This probable one-or two-hour interruption at the hospital would make that night even shorter.

As I made the fifteen-minute drive to and from the hospital on nearly deserted roads by mostly darkened houses, my slowly functioning mind kept coming back to this truth: Whereas freely chosen acts of self-denial have their place in any Christian's life, we should not forget the value of crosses that arise through the mere carrying out of daily duties.

During the first synod of Bishops at Rome in 1971, the assembled body discussed a document on "The Ministerial Priesthood." A sentence in this text expresses the concept that my mind kept pondering on that nocturnal trip to the hospital.

It says, "The renunciations imposed by the pastoral life itself help the priest to acquire an even greater sharing in Christ's Cross and hence a purer pastoral charity."

Those emergency sick calls immediately surface as examples because they usually occur at unexpected moments. This often puts stress upon us, especially if we happen at that very instant to be engaged in another important pastoral task. Moreover, the night time kind of summons I experienced obviously demands a "renunciation" and provides a "greater sharing in Christ's

Cross." But there are other challenges to our generosity as well, demands for service similar to, yet quite distinct from those which Dan and Laurie Roche encounter in their own professional and family lives.

• Mother Teresa of Calcutta is probably the best known contemporary servant of people who are in need. She founded her Missionaries of Charity with the expressed purpose, enshrined in their fourth vow, of "wholehearted and free service to the poorest of the poor."[4]

It began in 1952 when Mother Teresa picked up a man dying in the streets and being consumed by rats and ants. Mother Teresa found a home for him, and then for another dying person, and then for still another one. Today, forty years later, she along with her 3,000 sisters in 52 countries have cared for 42,000 people left in the streets. They have accomplished this, she says, by picking up abandoned people "one, by one, by one."

She walked by an open drain in Calcutta during those early days and discovered a dying man moving about in it. Mother Teresa took him back to a home where he could die surrounded by love and peace. The poor fellow told her, "I live like an animal in the streets. Now I will die like an angel."

This quite fragile-looking but very strong-willed nun has not been affected by her fame, which includes receiving the Nobel Peace Prize Award in 1979. She still goes barefoot when possible, sleeps on the floor of an open dormitory, eats lightly, uses only cold water from a pump, washes her own laundry, and owns only two white cotton outfits ("saris").

The motivating themes behind her life and the lives of her sisters are well known: Do "something beautiful for God"; "Give until it hurts"; "We do it for Jesus, to Jesus and with Jesus"; "We serve Jesus in the distressing disguise of the poor."[5]

• Pope John XXIII began his papal duties at an age when most people have long since retired. In addition to the enormous burdens that any pope must shoulder, this man, already in his seventh decade, conceived the notion of a Second Vatican Council and convened the bishops of the world for it.

However, three incidents at the end of his life when a fatal disease was ravaging his body epitomize the spirit of service that permeated the entire life of Angelo Roncalli.

He had worked hard to improve relations between the Vatican and the Italian government. Despite pain and weakness, Pope John pushed himself out of his sick bed and traveled to the Quirinale Palace in Rome for a formal visit with President Segni. The pope gave a short speech, embraced the president and said "For you and for Italy." One observer judges that this embrace finally brought about the sealing of a reconciliation between the Holy See and Italy.

The pope returned to the Vatican and collapsed on his bed. Later, while he was watching television coverage of the presidential meeting, the pope remarked: "A few hours ago I was being feted and complimented, and now I'm here alone with my pain. But that's all right; the first duty of a pope is to pray and suffer."[6]

About two weeks later, as the pope lay on his death bed, a bishop was about to minister the Church's Anointing of the Sick for him. Pope John XXIII sat up and spoke, acting in a sense as pastor, teacher, and servant even at that moment.

> The secret of my ministry is in that crucifix you see opposite my bed. It's there so that I can see it in my first waking moment and before going to sleep. It's there, also, so that I can talk to it during the long evening hours. Look at it, see it as I see it. Those open arms have been the programme of my pontificate: they say that Christ died for all, for all. No one is excluded from his love, from his forgiveness.[7]

Finally, at the start of this serious, fatal illness, the pope offered the pain, the anguish, and the very sacrifice of his life for the ecumenical council, for the Church and for all of humanity so longing for peace.[8] A pope is called "Servant of the Servants of the Lord." Pope John Paul XXIII lived that out until the very end.

Joy

Pam Panebianco does not impress visitors as a worried, sad, or burdened person. Despite her varied tasks and responsibilities as spouse, parent, and instructor, she radiates a certain peace and even joy.

This should not be surprising. Jesus and the Scriptures promise that. "Whoever loses his life for my sake will find it." "I have told you this so that my joy might be in you and your joy might be complete. This is my commandment: Love one another as I love you." "It is more blessed to give than to receive."[9]

I experienced such a joy among Mother Teresa's Missionaries of Charity. During 1976–77, as pastor-in-residence at the North American College in Rome, I alternated with other priests offering the daily morning Mass for her sisters in the outskirts of the city. Their formation house was located there by design. It was a modest complex beneath an ancient aqueduct surrounded by the huts and hovels of poor people who were simply trying to survive.

The fifty or so aspirants rise early, pray for an hour before the Blessed Sacrament, participate at Mass, have breakfast, and then leave for a day's work of various kinds with the poorest of the poor in the Eternal City. After their return at night, they spend another hour before the Lord in the tabernacle.

Despite the austerity of their living conditions and the rigors of their schedules, these women from all over the world clearly manifest an impressive sparkle, serenity, and joy.

Humility

"It is God's doing," Pam Panebianco remarked. "This task is bigger than we are." She and her husband Mike are convinced about the importance of their own teaching mission, but they also recognize that without God's guidance, strength, and grace, those efforts would bear little fruit. Their awareness echoes Jesus' words. "Just as a branch cannot bear fruit on its own unless it remains on the vine, so neither can you unless you remain in me. I am the vine, you are the branches. Whoever remains in me and I in him will bear much fruit, because without me you can do nothing."[10]

Sister of St. Joseph Barbara Ginter spent her life as a woman religious serving the poor and oppressed. She worked in several center-city parishes, organized people for effective action against injustices, spent a few years in Nicaragua, and frequently spoke to various groups about the need for Catholic Christians everywhere to be in solidarity with those who are hurting.

But then a fatal cancer altered her ministry from acting to suffering for others. On one occasion during the last stages of her terminal illness, she abruptly sat up and exclaimed to a friend next to her bed:

"I finally did it!"

This puzzled the companion by her side who asked for an explanation. Sister Barbara replied:

"I have always wanted to be in solidarity with the poor, to experience what it is to be helpless, totally dependent, and defenseless, to be powerless like the poor. But I have never achieved that. Now in the face of this disease over which I have no control, in the face of my imminent death, I finally know what it is to feel powerless like the poor."

When leaders have an attitude of personal powerlessness before the Lord and in face of responsibilities, then God can better act through them and, actually, transform them into exceedingly powerful persons.

Hope

To admit that a task or a duty is God's doing and bigger than we are reflects a real humility. However, it also can bespeak an unshakable hope. We may not be able to do anything without the Lord, but we are able to do all things in the Lord who strengthens us. If we believe that it is God's work which we are about, then we can likewise anticipate that God will provide us with what is needed to accomplish our task.

St. Paul experienced this double dimension of humility and hope. He begged God three times to be delivered of a burden. The Lord said, instead, "My grace is sufficient for you, for power is made perfect in weakness."

Paul then responded: "I will rather boast most gladly of my weaknesses, in order that the power of Christ may dwell with me. Therefore, I am content with weaknesses, insults, hardships, persecutions and constraints, for the sake of Christ; for when I am weak, then I am strong."[11]

John Cardinal O'Connor, the archbishop of New York, experienced in a bitterly painful way nearly three decades ago those humility and confidence, weakness and strength, and despair and hope combinations. He was serving with the Marine Corps in Okinawa and felt that he was losing his faith. He fought desperately to hold on to even the most fundamental of beliefs, belief in God's existence.

"We had a little Quonset hut chapel," Cardinal O'Connor recalls, "and night after night, after most of the troops were in their bunks, I would go into that chapel and kneel before the Blessed Sacrament and fight myself, almost as a man possessed, telling myself over and over and over again, 'Yes, the Son of God is here in this tabernacle, it's not just an empty set of beliefs!'

"I think it's as horrifying a feeling as one can possibly have—the threat of the loss of faith. During that period my favorite prayer became the cry of Christ on the Cross—'My God, my God, why hast thou forsaken me!' It was a period of incredible desolation.

"That was twenty-six years ago, and that passed, and since then I have been blessed extravagantly with faith that just overflows. But it has given me a great, great understanding and sense of compassion for those who experience that desolation and that sense of temptation."[12]

Whether it is a temptation with one's faith, a concern about some decisions, or a struggle with everyday duties, hope in the Lord's promised wisdom and strength provides peace and serenity.

Warm Welcoming

When couples come to the Panebianco home for instruction in NFP, Pamela and Michael try to welcome them warmly and to engage the entire family in extending that hospitality. The parents, of course, do the actual teaching and sharing, but the young children generally stay for awhile and help with the slide projector or video machine and serve refreshments. Their presence gives eloquent, even if unspoken testimony to the way in which this program fosters within the total family an open, informed, and healthy attitude toward sexuality as well as a strong bond of affection among family members.

That concern about gracious hospitality and a warm welcome for all reflects this famous command of Christ: "For I was hungry and you gave me food, I was thirsty and you gave me drink, a stranger and you welcomed me. . . ."[13] What we do to others, we are doing to the Lord as he appears to us, comes to us in his different disguises.

One Sunday morning during the 1970s, I flew from Syracuse to Chicago for a series of lectures that day in Joliet, Illinois. I was ensconced in my favorite right side, next to the aisle spot, when the flight attendant interrupted me to locate a handsome six-year-old boy next to the window, but separated from me by the empty middle seat.

We both buckled up and I returned to my personal reflections and prayer book. As the plane sped bumpily down the runway, I was stirred from my silent preoccupation by the sound of sobs. Turning to my youthful traveling companion, I noticed that his shoulders were heaving and gigantic tears were rolling down his face.

Not skilled at dealing with such crises, I reluctantly moved over to the lad, while grumbling to myself about the interruption.

His name was Jason. His single parent mother had just put him on the plane for a trip to Dallas and a visit to his grandmother. He had new clothes for school and a special hat for the journey. That start-up conversation took three minutes. What do I do now?

Fortunately, breakfast arrived. I tucked in his napkin, cut up the ham (he poured salt all over it), and watched as he covered the roll completely with butter. Breakfast was over and the tray gone in about fifteen minutes. I still had an hour with Jason before my deliverance in Chicago. What would be the next step?

The flight attendant came to my aid with a copy of *Ranger Rick*, not something I subscribe to at the rectory. I read a story to Jason from the magazine about a dog, a duck, and an oil spill on the East Coast—not a bad tale actually. Jason said I did all right, but his mother read better. To my relief, he then fell asleep.

When we landed at O'Hare airport, I moved back to Jason's side and explained:

"Jason, just like your mother promised, before lunchtime you will be in Dallas. Your grandmother will be there and you can run off the plane and meet her. But Jason, here is where I must get off."

He looked up at me with the saddest eyes, reminiscent of the boy in the movie *Champ*, and gave this questioning plea, "But who is going to take care of me now?"

In a relatively short period of time Jason would arrive in Dallas, run off the plane up the breezeway and leap into his grandmother's arms. He would then feel loved, cared for, important, significant, and content. But at that moment, as we parted, he felt abandoned, isolated, alone, not cared for, scared, unimportant, insignificant, and quite miserable.

In our broken, fragmented world today, the people who come to leaders often feel like Jason in his distress on the plane. After all, consider these facts: At least half of us today come from broken homes; by the age of eighteen, one-third of all women and one-fifth of all men have been sexually abused; moreover, personal and cultural insecurities and stress have driven many into destructive addictions. Leaders who welcome people warmly, who are humble, hopeful, and radiate joy, who recognize that service of others, caring about others, is their primary duty, can in many instances make troubled, hurting persons feel like Jason as he rushed from the plane and ran to his grandmother's embrace.

*A **Quote to Ponder:*** "Love cannot remain by itself—it has no meaning. Love has to be put into action and that action is service. . . . It is not how much we do, but how much love we put in the doing."[14]—Mother Teresa of Calcutta

*A **Biblical Role Model:*** The Apostles James and John with their mother made an ambitious request of Jesus. Christ responded with an admonition to them and their colleagues: Whoever wishes to be great must become a servant, like their master who came not to be served, but to serve.—Mark 10:35–45

A PERSPECTIVE

The story is told that Pope John XXIII, burdened by over eighty years of life and the heavy cares of the papacy, slowly walked each night to his private chapel for some time in prayer prior to retiring. His plea, however, was neither lengthy nor what we might expect. The jovial, but saintly man, it is said, prayed in this way, "Lord, it is your Church. I am going to bed."

That stance could be helpful for every leader—friend or colleague, parent or principal, pastor or president. For no leader possesses all of these qualities I have sketched; no leader has any of them to the desired degree; no leader uses them on every occasion with every person in precisely the correct way.

Leaders, therefore, following the example of John XXIII, might adopt an attitude that urges them simply to do their best and let God do the rest.

AN EXPLANATION

Specific case histories drawn from the actual experiences of others are always more meaningful than statements of abstract principles. For that reason, each chapter of Part II begins with a vignette, a look at a particular person whose life illustrates some aspect of the leadership experience.

These are neither flawless nor perfect people (assuming such can be found). And their leadership skills may not be limited to the one under discussion. But they do possess to some exceptional degree the characteristics treated in that chapter.

I looked for some leaders who would be known nationally and some who are recognized only by those with whom they are most immediately associated. I also sought for a roughly equal number of men and women. Finally, I aimed for nationwide representation.

Those were my goals. To achieve them I selected for interviews people with whom I had some connection, even if only by long-standing interest in their work. All but one person granted my request for an interview. Here is a brief explanation describing the process behind each of my choices.

William S. Norman: I have been a railroad fan from my earliest days and currently subscribe to several train journals. One issue carried a lengthy article on Amtrak's anniversary that featured interviews with some of its executives. In his remarks, Norman described his extensive efforts to develop a comprehensive marketing vision for Amtrak during the next decade.

Barbara and Francis Scholtz have been friends and colleagues of mine for more than a dozen years. I have been with them for their early morning prayer period, watched "Dutch" pull out his pocket Bible to read a few lines from the podium at a conference, and know they make an annual retreat.

Susan Champlin Taylor, my niece, is a very bright and energetic young woman. I have watched her grow up; I officiated at her wedding, worked with her on several writing projects, and baptized her first child. Without labeling them as such, she has in fact been making major personal and professional priority decisions for over a dozen years.

Lee Thomas. My interest in the Philadelphia Phillies baseball team dates back to my high school days when I attended a tryout camp in Utica, New York, and stayed on to watch a professional game that night. This was a very low-level league, but many of the team members eventually made the majors and even played in a World Series. The recent years have been difficult for the Phillies' organization. I have followed with keen interest Thomas' courageous and astute efforts to resurrect the franchise.

Roger Cardinal Mahony and I have been acquaintances for about two decades. I visited with him as the Cathedral rector in Fresno, corresponded with him as bishop of Stockton, met him here and there at conferences, and admired the massive information or idea-gathering project he initiated during his first months as archbishop of Los Angeles. His desire and ability to distinguish between the tip of the iceberg and the isolated ice cube were evident and impressive.

John D. Plumley and I were classmates and closest friends during our high school days at Camden Central School. Our different career and life directions kept our later contacts to a minimum, but there was always a bond between us. I watched Jack move gradually and wisely up the political ladder and felt great admiration for his keen skills in dealing with people. It was, however, only until our Labor Day interview that the connection between his family background, strong self-esteem, and comfort with others leapt out at me.

Patricia Livingston co-taught a course on listening skills to me and several dozen other church leaders at a workshop in New Jersey more than a dozen years ago. A personal and professional relationship grew from that initial encounter. We have often discussed the concepts in this book and used these ideas in separate and joint presentations to many audiences across the country.

Henry Mancini. I have always enjoyed this man's music and was delighted years ago, through my brother, to meet Mr. Mancini and his wife backstage at the Hollywood Bowl after a concert. My surface impression made me think that this artist had and has a unique ability to bring forth the best in other musicians. Visiting with him personally, observing him conduct at the Finger Lakes Performing Arts Center in Canandaigua, New York, and speaking with several members of two symphony orchestras which he had directed confirmed that original impression. Mr. Mancini was the first person to respond to my request for an interview. Moreover, he and Lisa, his office coordinator, could not have been more gracious and cooperative.

Sister Charla Commins, C.S.J. and I first connected some three decades ago when she was a Catholic high school student in Syracuse contemplating entrance into the religious life and I was a young associate priest at the Cathedral in that city providing her with spiritual direction. We have together worked through many personal, family, religious, and professional experiences since those days, the most recent of which has been the challenges of her position as director of a Catholic Charities social service agency.

Kathleen Bernardi with her husband and two children are members of St. Joseph's parish in Camillus. She has basically been a full-time mom for a decade, although she is now engaging in volunteer church work and contemplating a return to employment outside the home. It seemed critical to me that at least one of the vignettes feature a person who is *not* a well-known national or community leader and who has *not* gained distinction by unusual activity outside the home. Instead, that individual's leadership traits would have been demonstrated almost entirely in a domestic setting. This fact would highlight the notion that everyone is a leader, especially parents. Kathy seems to fulfill the role very well.

Thomas Wyman and I were classmates at Phillips Academy in Andover, Massachusetts. During the past twenty years his name has occasionally appeared in various contexts on the pages of *Time.* We exchanged notes after each appearance and later cooperated on a project in connection with our fortieth reunion at Andover. When the idea of interviewing leaders for this book emerged, Tom immediately came to my mind as a notable example of a leader in the corporate and communication world. His was my first interview. I left his New York office in the Olympia building elated by our exchange and excited by the positive contribution that and other interviews could offer the book.

Pamela Panebianco. Pam came to me when I was pastor of Holy Family Church in Fulton, New York with questions about Catholicism and, later, for instructions leading to her entrance into the church. I subsequently presided at her wedding and have maintained contact with Pam and her husband for the last fifteen years. It was my suggestion that originally brought them into contact with a Natural Family Planning physician. We have many times since discussed that topic and worked together on several related projects. I have seen Pam's leadership qualities firsthand both inside and outside the family.

NOTES

PART I · EVERYONE IS A LEADER

Chapter 1. Parents Especially

1. *Webster's Third New International Dictionary* (Springfield, Mass.: G. and C. Merriam Co., 1976), pp. 1282–1283.

PART II · HOW ANYONE CAN LEARN TO LEAD BETTER

1. Peter F. Drucker, *Managing the Non-Profit Organization* (New York: Harper/Collins, 1990), pp. 18, 21.

Chapter 1. Vision
1. An interview with William Norman at Union Station in Washington, D.C. on August 14, 1991.
2. *Time* magazine, November 9, 1987, "Who's in Charge," p. 18.
3. Henry Kissinger, quoted in Thomas J. Peters and Robert H. Waterman, Jr., *In Search of Excellence* (New York: Warner Books, 1984), p. 282.
4. John W. Gardner, "The Antileadership Vaccine," *Annual Report of the Carnegie Corporation* (New York: Carnegie Corporation, 1965), p. 12. Quoted in Warren Bennis and Burt Nanus, *Leaders* (New York: Harper and Row, 1985) , p. 215.
5. Bennis and Nanus, p. 103.
6. *Syracuse Herald-American*, December 22, 1991, "Clarke's Notepad," p. D-10.
7. William Safire and Leonard Safir, *Leadership* (New York: Simon and Schuster, 1990), p. 240.

Chapter 2. Reading and Reflection
1. An interview with Francis and Barbara Scholtz in Chicago on November 5, 1991.
2. See *General Instruction for the Liturgy of the Hours*, article 4 as quoted in

Joseph M. Champlin's, *Behind Closed Doors* (New York: Paulist Press, 1984), p. 180.

3. Dominique Lapierre, *The City of Joy* (New York: Warner Books, 1985), p.76. Roland Joffe's controversial film, *City of Joy*, made in Calcutta, was based very loosely on this book.

4. *Time* magazine, June 6, 1983, "Stress, Can We Cope," p. 52.

5. *Time* magazine, December 7, 1987, "New Age Harmonies," p. 69.

6. Henri Nouwen, *Clowning in Rome* (Garden City, N.Y.: Image Books, A Division of Doubleday and Company, 1979), p. 76.

Chapter 3. Priorities

1. Interview with Susan Champlin Taylor on August 28, 1991, in Los Angeles, California.

2. *Syracuse Herald-Journal*, "Wave of Emotions Follows Word of Chicago Church, School Closings." January 22, 1990, p. A5.

3. *The Christian Century*, March 18–25, 1987, p. 261.

4. *Time* magazine, "Drowsy America," December 17, 1990, pp. 78–85.

5. Ibid.

6. *Syracuse Herald-Journal*, "How Much Is Enough? Researchers Say Even Moderate Exercise Beneficial," November 28, 1988, B5, 7.

7. Ibid., B7.

8. Ibid.

9. Bishops' Committee on Priestly Life and Ministry, National Conference of Catholic Bishops, *The Health of American Catholic Priests: A Report and a Study* (Washington, D.C.: United States Catholic Conference, 1985), p. 50.

10. Ibid., p. 82.

11. Bishops' Committee on Priestly Life and Ministry, National Conference of Catholic Bishops, *The Priest and Stress* (Washington, D.C.: United States Catholic Conference, 1982), p. 21.

12. Lee Iacocca, *Iacocca: An Autobiography* (New York: Bantam Books, 1984), pp. 20–21.

Chapter 4. Courage

1. An interview with Lee Thomas in Philadelphia on August 12, 1991.

2. *USA TODAY Baseball Weekly*, September 13–19, 1991, pp. 3, 6.

3. *The Philadelphia Daily News*, September 5, 1991, p. 70.

4. *The Constitution on the Sacred Liturgy, Vatican Council II*, Austin Flannery, O.P., general editor (Northport, N.Y.: Costello Publishing Company, 1980), Article 21.

5. Alvin Toffler, *Future Shock* (New York: Random House, 1970), p. 13.

6. Ibid., pp. 297–300.

7. Elisabeth Kübler-Ross, *On Death and Dying* (New York: Macmillan, 1969).

8. *The Constitution on the Sacred Liturgy*, Article 23.

9. *Syracuse Herald-Journal*, "Mother Shocked at Killer's Release," January 31, 1992, p. B2.

10. *Syracuse Herald-Journal,* "Chittenango Suspends 9 Players," January 22, 1992, p. B10.

11. Written for a service in the Congregational church of Heath, Massachusetts, where Dr. Niebuhr spent many summers. The prayer was first printed in a monthly bulletin of the Federal Council of Churches. It became very popular with millions of copies in circulation and is the standard prayer for Alcoholics Anonymous and other similar recovery groups. Taken from John Bartlett, *Familiar Quotations* (Boston: Little, Brown and Company, 1980), p. 823.

Chapter 5. On Being a Target

1. An interview with Cardinal Roger Mahony and some staff members in Los Angeles, California, August 29, 1991.

2. John Naisbitt, *Megatrends* (New York: Warner Books, 1984), Chap. 7.

3. Acts of the Apostles, 1:13–14.

4. William Safire and Leonard Safir, *Leadership* (New York: Simon and Schuster, 1990), p. 228.

Chapter 6. Self-Esteem

1. An interview with John D. Plumley in Camden, New York, on September 2, 1991.

2. Robert Bauman, *The Gentleman from Maryland* (New York: Arbor House, 1986), p. 157.

3. Ibid., pp. 155–157.

4. Ibid., p.164.

5. A personal letter from Robert E. Bauman, September 8, 1987.

6. Bishops' Committee on Priestly Life and Ministry, National Conference of Catholic Bishops, *The Continuing Formation of Priests: Growing in Wisdom, Age and Grace* (Washington, D.C.: United States Catholic Conference, 1985), p. 13.

7. Donald P. McNeill, Douglas A. Morrison, Henri J. M. Nouwen, *Compassion* (Garden City, N.Y.: Doubleday and Company, 1982), p. 19.

8. John Eudes Bamberger, "Wrestling with God—The Merton We Knew," *Commonweal,* October 19, 1984, p. 556.

9. Patrick Carnes, Ph.D., *Out of the Shadows: Understanding Sexual Addiction* (Minneapolis: CompCare Publications, 1983), p. 120.

10. Gloria Steinem, *Revolution from Within* (Boston: Little, Brown and Company, 1992), pp. 5, 6, 9–10.

Chapter 7. Listening

1. An interview with Patricia Livingston in Camillus, New York, on October 18, 1991.

2. John W. Lawyer and Neil H. Katz, *Communication Skills for Ministry* (Dubuque, Iowa: Kendall/Hunt Publishing Company, 1985). Communication skills can only be taught and learned effectively in experiential settings and through actual practice, not by reading a book. However, this text does offer an excellent explanation of the theory behind good communication skills and many useful suggestions for carrying them out in daily circumstances.

3. *Time* magazine, August 21, 1989.

4. Warren Bennis and Burt Nanus, *Leaders* (New York: Harper and Row, 1985), p. 96.

Chapter 8. Empowering

1. An interview with Henry Mancini in Saratoga Springs, New York, on August 13, 1991.

2. *Syracuse New Times*, July 17–24, 1991, pp. 1, 6.

3. Herman Wouk, *War and Remembrance* (New York: Pocket Books, 1980), p. 701.

4. Ibid.

5. Tom Peters and Nancy Austin, *A Passion of Excellence* (New York: Random House, 1985), p. xix.

Chapter 9. Affirming

1. Interview with Sister Charla Commins, C.S.J. on August 12 and 31, 1991, in Saratoga Springs and Syracuse, New York.

2. Thomas J. Peters and Robert H. Waterman, Jr., *In Search of Excellence* (New York: Warner Books, 1984), pp. 70–71.

3. Ibid., p. 58.

4. J. Stanley Coyne, *The Wind at My Back* (Utica, N.Y.: North Country Books, 1992), chapter 2. Also, a personal conversation with Coyne on December 6, 1991, at Liverpool, New York.

5. From *Bits and Pieces* (Fairfield, N.J.: The Economics Press, 1991), vol. M/ no. 10, p. 7.

Chapter 10. Evaluating Others — And Yourself

1. An interview with Kathleen Bernardi in Camillus, New York, on May 4, 1992.

2. Emmanuel Heufelder, *The Way to God: According to the Rule of St. Benedict* (Kalamazoo, Mich.: Cistercian Publications, 1983), p. 291.

3. John W. Lawyer and Neil H. Katz, *Communications Skills for Ministry* (Dubuque, Iowa: Kendall/Hunt Publishing Company,1985), Chap. 5.

4. Kenneth Blanchard and Spencer Johnson, *The One Minute Manager* (New York: Berkley Publishing Group, 1983), pp. 50–62.

5. Quoted in William Barclay, *The Daily Bible Series: The Letters to the Corinthians* (Philadelphia: The Westmaster Press, 1975), p. 37.

Chapter 11. Excellence

1. From an interview with Thomas H. Wyman in New York City on August 8, 1991.

2. Thomas J. Peters and Robert H. Waterman, *In Search of Excellence* (New York: Warner Books, 1984), p. 5.

3. Ibid.

4. Ibid.

5. Richard Justice, "Clark Doesn't Try to Temper Success," *Washington Post*, August 4, 1991, D-1, 5.

Chapter 12. On Being a Servant
1. An interview with Pamela Keller Panebianco at Skaneateles, New York, in August 1991.
2. John 15:12, 15:13; Matthew 20:28.
3. Tom Clancy, *The Sum of All Fears* (New York: G.P. Putnam's Sons, 1991), p. 76.
4. Eileen Egan, *Such a Vision of the Street* (Garden City, N.Y.: Doubleday and Company, 1985), p. 135.
5. Mother Teresa, *Words to Love By* . . . (Notre Dame, Ind.: Ave Maria Press, 1983), pp. 5–7.
6. Peter Hebblethwaite, *Pope John Paul XXIII* (Garden City, N.Y.: Doubleday and Company, 1985), p. 494.
7. Ibid., p. 501.
8. Ibid., p. 500.
9. Matthew 10:39; John 15:11–12; Acts 20:35.
10. John 15:4–5.
11. 2 Corinthians 12:9–10.
12. Leslie Bennetts, "God's Man in New York," *Vanity Fair*, August, 1990, p. 161.
13. Matthew 25:31–46.
14. Mother Teresa, *Words to Love By* . . . . p. 75.